TALES OF THE SILVER COAST

Brunswick County

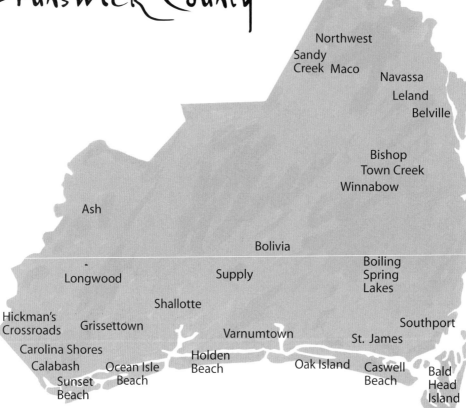

Northwest

Sandy
Creek Maco

Navassa

Leland

Belville

Bishop
Town Creek
Winnabow

Ash

Bolivia

Boiling
Spring
Lakes

Longwood

Supply

Shallotte

Hickman's
Crossroads

Grissettown

Varnumtown

Southport

St. James

Carolina Shores

Calabash

Ocean Isle
Beach

Holden
Beach

Oak Island

Caswell
Beach

Bald
Head
Island

Sunset
Beach

Incorporated towns and communities mentioned in the text

TALES OF THE SILVER COAST

A Secret History of North Carolina's Brunswick County

MILLER POPE

with Jacqueline DeGroot

Illustrated by the author

Tales of the Silver Coast: A Secret History of North Carolina's Brunswick County
© 2006 Miller Pope
Published by Winoca Press
106 North 16th Street
Wilmington NC 28401
www.winocapress.com

Cover and interior design: Nicki Leone
Cover illustration: photo by Miller Pope; map illustration based on Sauthier's 1769 map of
Brunswick Town.
Interior illustrations and photos by Miller Pope except where noted. Thanks to the following
for permission to reproduce their images: Ken Buckner, pp. 100,104,105 (top), 131,132; Bobby
Williamson, pp. 74, 77, 79; Brunswick Electric Membership Corporation, pp. 80-82; Atlantic
Telephone Membership Corporation, pp. 83, 84; Barbara Brannon, pp. 113, 122; U.S. Geological
Survey, 125

Printed in Canada
09 08 07 06   5 4 3 2 1

LIBRARY OF CONGRESS CATALOGING-IN-PUBLICATION DATA

Pope, Miller.
  Tales of the silver coast : a secret history of North Carolina's Brunswick County /
Miller Pope, with Jacqueline DeGroot ; illustrated by the author.
     p. cm.
     ISBN-13: 978-0-9755910-8-6
     ISBN-10: 0-9755910-8-8
  1. Brunswick County (N.C.)—History—Anecdotes. I. DeGroot, Jacqueline. II. Title.
     F262.B9P66 2006
     975.6′29—dc22
                    2006008777

To Helen

CONTENTS

PART I: FIVE CENTURIES ON THE SILVER COAST
Brunswick Then and Now

PART II: SETTLERS, SAILORS, AND SOLDIERS
The Struggle for Conquest of Land and Sea

PART III: PLANTATIONS AND PROGRESS
Commerce along the Southeastern Coast

PART IV: THE WEIRD AND THE WONDERFUL
A Few Brunswick Tales Worth Retelling

PART V: LOGGERHEADS AND LIGHTHOUSES
Brunswick's Beaches and Waterways

PART VI: EXPLORING THE SILVER COAST TODAY
Sights and Sites in Brunswick and Beyond

Preface

When my wife and I first decided to move south to North Carolina's Brunswick County in the early 1970s, neighbors from our suburban New York community of Westport, Connecticut, asked, with no little concern on their faces, "But who will you *talk* to?"

Our Yankee friends seriously underestimated the welcoming nature of our new community in then-rural southeastern North Carolina. They didn't know what delights we would discover in Brunswick County's silver-sand beaches, sparkling waters, and temperate climate. And they understood nothing of the serene natural beauty of the place, much less its storied history and its intriguing tales of pirates and soldiers, fishers and farmers, patriots and rebels—all manner of characters grandiose and simple.

Even today, when Brunswick's waterways and former pastures are sprouting homes and businesses like weeds and its population has been swelled both by newcomers from afar and other North Carolinians heading east, many residents and visitors haven't discovered these fascinating stories. The tales of our Silver Coast have been a secret to them.

And so it is the purpose of this book to be more than just a brief history of Brunswick County. (Others have offered up more comprehensive, or more scholarly, accounts.) It is an attempt to introduce the reader to the feel and flavor of this wonderful paradise.

In these pages you won't find a systematic, year-by-year analysis of the political, social, or economic events that made Brunswick County what it is today. You won't find a transcription of every relevant historical document or an official biography of important figures. What you will find is the story behind the textbook, or the historical marker, or the name of a place or town. You'll encounter a few curiosities of our county and region as well. I've enjoyed telling them—and I hope you enjoy reading them.

This project began at the suggestion of Anne Harris and Patricia Wilson of the Pelican Bookstore at Sunset Beach. Over my many years as a graphic designer and commercial illustrator, I collaborated on scores of book projects, including school textbooks and encyclopedias, and illustrated magazines during the "golden age of illustration"—but I had never until now written a book.

I began to compile many of the local tales I have heard from the past two decades, and to write down what I have learned from visits to sites around the county, both well-known and obscure. The episodes I chose to include follow no rigid pattern—they simply reflect things I found fascinating, and I expected others would, too. Many of them are stories presented in an earlier version in the newsletter we published for guests at The Winds resort in Ocean Isle Beach.

Helen Otis Pope

I have used several important resources to check facts and supply details. Lawrence Lee's *History of Brunswick County, North Carolina* (1980) remains the standard reference, though it is long out of print. Bill Reaves compiled two useful volumes of history as *Southport: A Chronology* (vol. 1, 1520–1887, pub. 1978; vol. 2, 1887–1920, pub. 1990). The websites of the Brunswick County Library (http://library.brunsco.net), North Carolina Historic Sites/Brunswick Town (www.ah.dcr.state.nc.us/sections/hs/brunswic/brunswic.htm), and Orton Plantation Gardens (www.ortongardens.com) are quite informative, as is the New Hanover Public Library's article "Facts and Firsts: History of the Lower Cape Fear" (www.co.new-hanover.nc.us/LIB/history/lhcfhist.asp). Genealogist J. D. Lewis provides a wealth of information on southeastern North Carolina on his website (www.carolana.com/brunswick_county_nc.html). Interesting information on Brunswick political figures may be found at The Political Graveyard (www.politicalgraveyard.com).

I have also relied on the assistance of Brunswick County author Jacqueline DeGroot in researching and writing portions of the book. In later stages Barbara Brannon and Nicki Leone lent their expertise to copyediting, fact-checking, and design. As in any work of history, errors may unintentionally survive into print; I welcome feedback from readers who may feel they have spotted possible inaccuracies.

The illustrations I have selected for this book reflect my own enjoyment of local scenes and my quest for history. While some were produced by traditional methods, many were produced in a digital "studio," painted with a digital brush or pen. Some are based on photographic images. Many of the base images are my own; others are well-known historical documents. Some of the scenes are simply products of my imagination.

My late wife, Helen, was an ardent Carolinian by adoption. Her love for Brunswick County and coastal North Carolina was as genuine as a native's, and she made it her cause to learn about the region and tell others about it. It was Helen who coined the term we now universally apply to our part of coast, "The South Brunswick Islands." Helen would have appreciated this book of history and legend. I dedicate it to her memory.

Miller Pope

TALES OF THE SILVER COAST

A Secret History of North Carolina's Brunswick County

FIVE CENTURIES
ON THE SILVER COAST
Brunswick Then and Now

The Cape Fear River, the longest of North Carolina's major river systems contained entirely within the state, forms the eastern boundary of Brunswick County as it empties into the Atlantic Ocean between Southport and Bald Head Island. Here at the site of Old Brunswick Town and Fort Anderson, the river is about a mile wide. OVERLEAF: An alley of live oaks at Orton Plantation.

The Making of Brunswick County

BRUNSWICK COUNTY OCCUPIES THE southernmost corner of North Carolina and contains some of the country's most beautiful marshes and water views, as well rural farmland that is both verdant and bucolic. It is one of the state's largest counties in land area, and one of its fastest growing in population. Thousands of years ago Brunswick County was completely covered by the sea—it remains only a few feet above sea level today.

Brunswick County is unique in that its southern shore is situated at the same latitude as Los Angeles. It lies south of all of South Carolina's major cities except Charleston and Myrtle Beach. And it enjoys a winter climate hardly different from that of the states farther south.

The Brunswick County shoreline is made up of pristine, sandy beaches lined with beautiful beach homes. Rows of houses, both elegant and cottagey, stand tall in the sun, buffered by grass-covered dunes. The mainland, and the deep interior of the county, is a virtual wilderness and home to alligators, bear, deer, and carnivorous plants. Bird sanctuaries abound, the species too numerous to name here.

Exploring Chicora

Giovanni da Verrazano arrived at or near Cape Fear in early March 1524. He then sailed northward, exploring the eastern seaboard of North America all the way to Nova Scotia. His discoveries included New York Bay, Block Island, and Narragansett Bay. He was the first European to name new discoveries of North American sites after Old World persons and places.

THE NATIVE PEOPLES OF THE REGION, INDIANS related to the Waccamaw and the Choctaw, called this area Chicora. Today, whether as an allusion to later pirate activity on these shores or an image of its sparkling sands, we sometimes refer to it as the Silver Coast.

In 1524 Giovanni da Verrazano, an Italian exploring on behalf of the King of France, landed on the coast of or near Brunswick County. He was the county's first European visitor—but certainly not the last.

Only two years later, Lucas Vásquez de Ayllón, a Spaniard, arrived in Chicora with the intent of establishing a colony. He entered a large river situated at latitude 33 degrees, 40 minutes, which he named "Rio Jordan." His bearings are taken by many as evidence that he had discovered the Cape Fear River.

But the Spanish did not press their advantage in the region, and the English sought to establish settlements on the coast a bit farther north. In 1629 King Charles I

An early eighteenth-century Charles Town (Charleston) gentleman. Brunswick Town was founded by settlers from the island of Barbados, arriving by way of Charles Town in South Carolina.

of England granted what today comprises North and South Carolina to his attorney general, Sir Robert Heath, and named it Carolana (derived from the Latin for Charles) in honor of himself. But Heath never attempted to settle a colony in the new world, and his grant was later declared invalid. King Charles II, in 1663, subsequently expanded and regranted this vast territory to a group of eight of his supporters, nobles who were given the title of Lords Proprietors. The new grant was called Carolina, again in honor of Charles I. The Lords Proprietors ruled irregularly as absentees, and seven of them eventually sold their grants (including what is now Brunswick County) to the British crown in 1729.

King Charles I of England awarded the first land grants in the territory he called Carolana (derived from his own name) and that today comprises North and South Carolina.

The First Charles Town

IN 1662 ENGLISHMAN WILLIAM Hilton, exploring on behalf of the Massachusetts Bay Colony, spent considerable time in Carolina, trading with the Cape Fear Indians and establishing friendly relations. Hilton's travels ranged far to the south (where Hilton Head Island, South Carolina, is named for him) and deep into the interior of Carolina. He reached the Cape Fear River in August 1662, calling it "Charles River." The following year Hilton returned to the area, just ahead of a group of settlers from New England who had been persuaded by Hilton's first voyage. John Vassall, representing a group of planters from Barbados, also brought settlers to Clarendon County, as the Brunswick area was originally called. Vassall's group established Charles Town on the west bank of the Cape Fear about twenty miles

Edward Moseley's "A New and Correct Map of the Province of North Carolina," 1733, shows "Port Brunswick or Cape Fear Harbour" as part of Clarendon County. Courtesy Joyner Library, East Carolina University.

inland, near the mouth of Town Creek (or "Indian River," as Hilton had called it). This first "Charles Town" in the Carolinas was settled decades before the city of that name far to the south!

The European population of the Lower Cape Fear area grew to more than 800 people within two years. But by 1667, however, the colonists had become disillusioned. The harshness of the wilderness and conflicts with the local Indians made life difficult for them. Pirates were also a constant threat. To top it off, the Lords Proprietors closed their Carolina land-office—and the Europeans deserted their holdings in Clarendon County.

Settlement of the Lower Cape Fear area resumed in earnest after threats of pirates and hostile Indians, and establishment of a more reliable government, improved conditions. In the mid-eighteenth century Brunswick Town was small, but in its heyday it was a busy port and home to a number of prosperous merchants.

Other Early Settlers

FOR THE NEXT HALF A CENTURY, DURING which time Carolina came to be divided into North and South sections, there was little effort by the English to reestablish a colony in the Lower Cape Fear region. In 1714 Thomas James received a grant of 1,000 acres on the western side of the Cape Fear River and settled there, but a year later he and his family were found murdered by natives.

Genealogical records indicate that around 1724 a Jacob Johnson and his wife, Ann, lived in the area briefly but illegally, without the right of a land grant from the Lords Proprietors.

The earliest legal grant on record in the area conveys Barren Island (later Smith Island; now Bald Head Island) and most of present-day Southport to Landgrave Thomas Smith, a wealthy planter from South Carolina, on May 8, 1713.

Concerted efforts to rid the coast of pirates, combined with the defeat of hostile natives during the Tuscarora Wars and improvement in provincial governance, again made the Lower Cape Fear safe for exploration and colonization. Settlement resumed in earnest after Gov. George Burrington made land grants in June 1725 to Eleazer Allen, Charles Harrison, Maurice Moore, and Samuel Swann.

George, Prince Elector of Hanover and Duke of Brunswick, succeeded to the English throne upon the death of Queen Anne, the last of the Stuart line, none of whose eighteen children had survived to adulthood. King George I, as he became, spoke almost no English— but the title of his dukedom lives on in the name of North Carolina's southernmost county.

The most visible structure from Brunswick's earliest days is St. Philip's Anglican Church. Its surviving walls date back to 1754, when the Anglican parish of St. Philip began building a brick church at Brunswick, the seat of royal government in the colony. The church was finally completed in 1768 after a financial struggle and a destructive hurricane. In 1776, only a few years later, it was burned by the British. Today, only a rectangular shell remains of St. Philip's Church.

The Fortunes of Brunswick Town

MAURICE MOORE LENT HIS CONSIDERABLE ingenuity and determination to developing a viable economy out of hostile swamps and thickly forested land. In 1726 Moore founded Brunswick Town on a quiet, picturesque site on the west bank of the Cape Fear River, naming it in honor of King George I of England, a native of Brunswick, Germany. Brunswick Town became the seat of New Hanover County, which was established in 1729 and named in honor of England's alliance with the German house of Hanover. The newly formed county encompassed many other present-day counties, including Brunswick.[1]

But Brunswick Town was little more than a frontier outpost. In April 1733, a group of landowners upriver began laying out a town on the east bank and selling lots. Originally called New Carthage, the upstart town was also called New Liverpool, New Town, or Newton. By 1735 the royal governor had ordered the county court to begin meeting at Newton rather than Brunswick Town, and in 1740 Newton was incorporated as the Town of Wilmington and designated as the new county seat.

The switch so angered the original settlers on the west side of the Cape Fear River that they launched a campaign to secede from New Hanover County that would last for decades. Friction between the opposing sides of the river did not cease when Brunswick was given its own parish, St. Philip's, which in 1741 incorporated all lands west of the Cape Fear River.

On March 9, 1764, the region was officially removed from New Hanover County and combined with part of Bladen County to establish Brunswick County, and Brunswick Town was restored to its status as a county seat. It would hold that distinction until 1779.

"King" Roger Moore (1694–1759), founder of Orton Plantation, was so called on account of his imperious disposition. He purchased the Orton property from his elder brother, Maurice, and built the first residence there in 1725. Handsome statuary adorns the gates at the entrance.

The Brunswick County town of Shallotte owes its existence to a ferry and later a bridge over the Shallotte River. (Photo illustration based on Lee, *History of Brunswick County*, p. 120ff)

Growth, Industry, and Dissent
in Colonial Times

The American colonists came to detest the British stamp they were required to purchase as a tax to support the mother country. In Brunswick and along the Cape Fear in 1765, the colonists rose up in protest and defeated this form of taxation.

Brunswick's fortunes grew throughout the early eighteenth century. Brunswick Town had became a thriving seaport for exporting naval stores—tar, pitch, and turpentine derived from the resin of the longleaf pine. The Royal Navy and the British mechant fleet that plied the oceans between Europe, the colonies, and the islands of the Caribbean required this "sticky gold" for building and maintaining the great wooden oceangoing ships of the day. The sap from North Carolina pine trees was as necessary to commerce in the age of sail as petroleum is today.

In 1765—eight years before the Boston Tea Party—the American colonists challenged the British crown's authority to distribute the despised tax stamps. Throughout the colonies, local representatives of the crown forced merchants to pay taxes on official port functions and shipping costs. In Brunswick and along the Cape Fear, the colonists protested and effectively prevented collection of the tax. It was the first organized act of rebellion in the colonies' move toward independence. The royal governor was almost powerless to stem the tide lest he ignite a firestorm.

Naval stores from Southeastern North Carolina forests—tar, pitch, and turpentine from the abundant longleaf pine—helped create the naval might of the British Empire.

Though the people of eighteenth-century Brunswick had access to imports from other colonies and across the sea, most tools, clothing, and foodstuffs were homemade.

Brunswick Town had gained political significance as well. Two successive royal governors resided in Brunswick; the town functioned as a political center, and the colonial assembly occasionally met in its courthouse. But Brunswick Town was dealt a blow in 1770 when the seat of the royal governor was moved to New Bern, more than a hundred miles to the north.

Completed in 1854, the Brunswick County Courthouse building that serves today as Southport's City Hall replaced an earlier single-story structure. In the days when travel in the county had been largely by boat, Southport had been a convenient location, but with the advent of better roads a large part of the population wanted the county government situated more centrally, and the county seat was moved to Bolivia in 1975.

Brunswick in the Early Republic

AFTER THE REMOVAL OF THE ROYAL GOVERNOR, the town began to decline. Other factors, including the growth of nearby Wilmington (Newton), also contributed to the eclipse of Brunswick's role. By the spring of 1776, when British Redcoats came ashore from the Royal Navy ship *Cruizer*, the town's population had decreased substantially. Reports indicate that a large part of the town was burned during this raid. By the end of the Revolutionary War, most families and merchants had moved to other locations. The latter half of the war, fought primarily in the South, had been especially brutal on the residents of the region. A portion of Brunswick's residents had remained loyal to the king and supported the British—but these loyalists found all of their property confiscated after the war.

In 1779, the town of Lockwood Folly was named Brunswick's county seat. Court convened there at the house of John Bell until a courthouse was built in 1786. The county seat was moved yet again in 1808, to Smithville (present-day Southport), a river pilots' town at the mouth of the Cape Fear River established in 1792. Southport would remain the county seat until 1975. The original county seat of Brunswick Town was incorporated into Roger Moore's Orton Plantation in 1842.

An eighteenth-century British navy sloop-of-war, a small warship with a single gun deck that carried as many as eighteen cannon.

Brunswick Town During the Civil War

SOME TWENTY YEARS LATER THE SITE OF BRUNSWICK Town once again entered the forefront of history, playing a minor but crucial role in the Civil War. The Cape Fear River was a vital entry point for ships running the Union blockade to the port of Wilmington, from which supplies moved by rail to Petersburg and on to Richmond for General Lee's army.

To aid in river defense, the Confederate army constructed a large sand fortification originally called Fort St. Philip's, soon renamed Fort Anderson. It consisted of two five-cannon batteries overlooking the shipping channel to provide protection to blockade runners.

After the fall of Fort Fisher at the mouth of the river in February 1865, Union forces attacked Fort Anderson from both the land and the river. After three days of fierce fighting, the Confederates slipped out of the fort at night. At daybreak Union gunboats began firing, unaware that it was their own soldiers breaching the walls of the fort. The Federal infantry frantically waved sheets and blankets in an attempt to stop the deadly rain of fire from their own guns. The guns fell silent, and the site that had once been a thriving colonial city once again slipped into obscurity.

North Carolina provided more troops to the Confederacy during the Civil War than any other state; Brunswick County, due to its strategic location at the mouth of the Cape Fear River, played a key role for both North and South during the war.

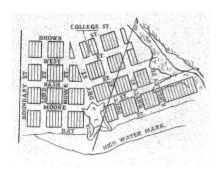

The original town plan of Smithville (Southport) shows the layout of neatly arranged streets centered around Fort Johnston, on the waterfront. This map is carved onto a stone located at Southport's waterfront.

Townships, Towns, and Communities

FROM THE TIME OF ITS FOUNDING BRUNSWICK County has been divided into a number of administrative districts. Six such districts were organized in 1812: Lockwood Folly, Northwest, Shallotte, Smithville, Town Creek, and Waccamaw, all of which remain active townships today.

Following the initiative of Brunswick Town in 1726, other settlements began to arise around the county. Lockwood Folly sprang up and thrived for a while, but after its brief stint as the county seat it quickly faded into oblivion. Today it comprises a small residential and recreational community on the Lockwood Folly River.

Records show that by 1734 there was a settlement near the ferry crossing of the Little Charlotte River called Little Charlotte. Old maps of this area, as early as 1747, labeled the waterway the Shallot River. A bridge had replaced the ferry by 1807, and soon the place name seems to have taken on its modern form as well. By the 1830s the community was known as Shallotte. A post office was established in 1837, and the town of Shallotte (nowadays pronounced shuh-LOAT) was incorporated in 1899.

Early roads in the county were mostly sand and nearly impassable. Travel by boat was there-

Until well into the twentieth century, Brunswick County's roads were unpaved, sandy tracks, and mules and oxen were numerous.

fore the only practical way to go. In the 1820s a trading post was established on the Lockwood Folly River, near the road between Wilmington and Shallotte. This trading post was originally called the "Old Georgetown Way" (to Georgetown, South Carolina) before being shortened to "Old G.W." It was finally renamed Supply by the locals in the 1860s.

Inland, other small towns arose around crossroads, streams, railroad stops, and fishing villages. Many were named after large plantations or their owners, or other famous citizens—the source of some of these names is a matter of dispute. Exum, Ash, Longwood, Grissettown, and Thomasboro sprang up, and Calabash and Hickman's Crossroads soon joined them. On the northern end of the county, Maco, Bishop, Leland, Belville, and Winnabow grew into towns.

The town of Bolivia was established in the 1890s and incorporated in 1911. Despite much heated controversy, in 1975 Brunswick's county seat was moved from Southport to Bolivia. Many citizens felt that because of its more central location Bolivia could provide better service to the population.

Close to the tip of the Cape Fear River lies Southport. Southport is home to fewer than 3,000 souls who love their quaint and quiet town. It was founded to house the pilots who still guide big ships, coming from all over the world, up the Cape Fear River and into the port of Wilmington.

There isn't much to do in this sleepy little town unless you like boats, deep sea fishing, art galleries, or antique shops—except to drink in the atmosphere and just relax under the Spanish moss. It is truly a beautiful city, Americana at its best.

Life and Leisure in Present-Day Brunswick County

ONE MAJOR PUBLIC PROJECT LED TO THE CREATION of several of Brunswick's towns. In the 1930s the U.S. Army Corps of Engineers dredged the North Carolina portions of the Maine-to-Florida Inland Waterway (later Intracoastal Waterway). On the Brunswick County shore the waterway created several new "barrier islands," which became attractive properties in the years following World War II.

Inland Brunswick was still rural, a rustic counterpart to bustling Wilmington across the river, for most of the twentieth century. US Highway 17, connecting Wilmington and the beach resorts of Myrtle Beach, South Carolina, traversed the entire length of the county, mostly through swampland and pine forest. Highway 74/76 crossed Brunswick into Columbus County, through similar scenery. After World War II the Brunswick River, a tidal tributary of the Cape Fear, was used as a scuttling site for mothballed navy vessels, and their rusting hulks marked the riverbank near the highway into Wilmington well into the 1960s.

North Carolina pine trees were "boxed" in the winter so that raw turpentine could be collected in the spring. This "sticky gold" provided the turpentine and pitch so vital to Britain's—and later America's—shipbuilding industries and naval power.

Development got into full swing in the 1950s, and in the 1960s the beachfront communities began to boom. Since the 1950s Sunset Beach, Ocean Isle Beach, Holden Beach, Oak Island, and Caswell Beach have all been become towns; today they are tremendous vacation attractions. Boiling Spring Lakes, Bald Head Island, and St. James, near Southport, have all been developed as resort towns.

Little towns have been created at such a rapid rate in

LEFT: The building reputed to be Brunswick County's first schoolhouse with glass windows was built in 1856. There was no formal school system in the county until the late nineteenth century. (Photo illustration based on Lee, *History of Brunswick County,* p. 120ff)

Brunswick County, that today it has more towns than any other county in the state. Brunswick, which was one of the poorest counties in the state, now abounds with posh gated golf communities and beach resorts.

Though prosperity is by no means universal in the county, Brunswick's greatly increased tax base has provided for civic and infrastructure improvements that benefit all. The term "Silver Coast" takes on yet another layer of meaning as Brunswick's desirability as a place to live and work brings growing good fortune to the historic county.

In distilleries throughout the backwoods, turpentine was distilled from the sap of pine trees.

Today Brunswick is known for its "silver coast" of beachfront and sparkling water as much as for the "sticky gold" of its naval stores industries or its pirates' treasure.

Brunswick County today boasts some of the best golfing in the nation, with a temperate climate year-round and more than two dozen superb courses. The course shown here is at Sea Trail Plantation, a resort community at Ocean Isle Beach.

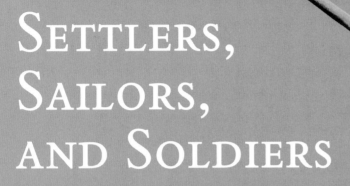

SETTLERS, SAILORS, AND SOLDIERS

the Struggle
for Conquest of Land
and Sea

Tuscarora Indians whose descendants today live in New York State once roamed Brunswick County. OVERLEAF: During the Revolutionary period, Tories and Patriots clashed on Brunswick soil.

The First Carolinians

IN A TIME WHEN SCIENTIFIC STUDY has taught us a great deal about earlier civilizations, we know relatively little about Southeastern North Carolina's original inhabitants. The indigenous peoples of the region were relatively isolated. Today, sandy soils make archeology difficult. But researchers believe that native Americans arrived in the Cape Fear area by at least 10,000 B.C.

Shell middens found on nearby Bald Head Island, where Indians left the remains of their oystering and shellfishing, have been dated back eight hundred years. When the Italian explorer Giovanni Da Verrazano visited the area in March 1524, sailing for Francis I of France, he found the natives friendly. "They go nude of everything," Verrazano wrote in his report to the king on July 8, 1524, "except that at the private parts they wear some skins of little animals . . . a girdle of fine grass woven with various tails of other animals which hang around the body as far as the knees; the rest nude; the head likewise.

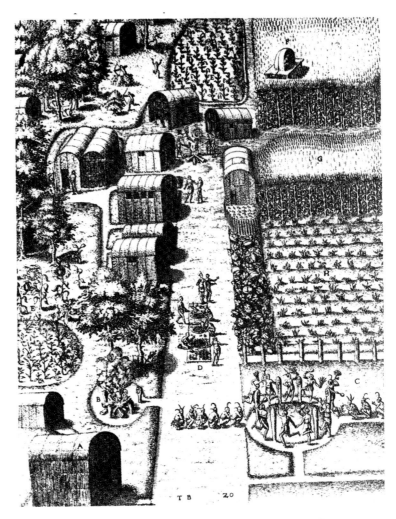

Early Carolina explorer John White's drawing from the 1580s was one of the most accurate depictions of Native American settlements on the Carolina coast. (Engraving from Theodor de Bry's *America*, 1590)

Some wear certain garlands of feathers of birds."

Scholars believe these people were the Cape Fear Indians, who inhabited the river areas in present-day Brunswick and New Hanover Counties.

Like their northern neighbors, the Croatans, the Cape Fear Indians probably relied heavily on coastal estuaries for food, seining the sounds for small fish and collecting oysters and clams. The Cape Fear Indians might have hunted extensively in coastal swamplands, stalking deer, bear, turkeys, and game birds with bow and arrow.

When Capt. William Hilton scouted the area for the English colonists from Barbados in 1662, he visited Necroes, a Cape Fear village in Brunswick County about twenty miles north of the river's mouth. The Indians seemed eager to trade, offering a variety of fish and acorns. This festival of friendship climaxed on December 1, 1663, when the chief Wat-Coosa deeded the river and contiguous lands to the English settlers. The chief even gave the English two of his daughters to cement the deal.

Headdress of a Tuscarora Indian

From this point, however, American history slipped into a pattern it would often repeat. Disease introduced by the white explorers accounted for dreadful loss, and wars between the Indians themselves were made worse by the introduction of the white men's firearms. In 1715, Col. Maurice Moore and a force of Tuscaroras, heading to fight the Yamassee Indians in South Carolina, detoured to fight the Waccamaws and the Cape Fear Indians, driving most of them from the region.

The Yamassee War largely finished the native Americans in coastal North Carolina. Most of the Cape Fear Indians migrated into South Carolina. In southeastern North Carolina, traveler Hugh Meredith reported to Benjamin Franklin in 1730, "There is not an Indian to be seen in this Place."

Not all Indian presence was eradicated, though. Many native American groups survived, apparently by moving inland through the Green Swamp into counties where their descendants can be found in large numbers today.

The Museum of Coastal Carolina on Ocean Isle Beach devotes an entire section to the first inhabitants of this region, with many artifacts found in the immediate area. It is well worth a trip to see some of its wonderful exhibits.

History Buff Heaven

THERE ARE FEW PLACES IN AMERICA that can offer the variety of historical sites virtually on the doorstep of everyone in Brunswick County. For instance, the European history of this area goes back nearly five hundred years—to 1524, when Verrazano made landfall, only two years after Cortez conquered Mexico!

A few more of Brunswick's historical highlights:

In 1526 Lucas Vásquez de Ayllón arrived at Cape Fear with six hundred settlers. The exact site of the colony, which lasted only a few months, has yet to be identified.

Further settlements tried and failed; the Cape Fear Indians were hostile and pirates were plentiful. By 1720 the Indians had been defeat-

British soldiers of the American Revolution

ed and the most notorious of the pirates had been captured.

Brunswick Town, only an archeological excavation today, was founded by 1726 and the area began to thrive.

From these beginnings the lower Cape Fear Area went on to play a significant part in the events leading up to the American Revolution, such as the Stamp Act Rebellion, and the revolution itself.

The history of the Brunswick area reverberates with raids by Spanish fleets, British invasions, bombardments, and assaults by Union fleets.

Fortifications from most of America's wars are found in Brunswick County (one, Fort Johnston, even predates the founding of our nation).

Famous military names are associated with this little corner of the world. Lord Cornwallis; the "Swamp Fox," Francis Marion; Stede Bonnet, "The Gentleman Pirate," are but a few. George Washington even paid Brunswick a visit in 1791, staying overnight in the Gause Plantation House, which stood at Gause Landing.

Whether you are an avid history buff or just casually interested in American history, when you're in Brunswick County you have only to look—history is all around you. Many a town, many a house, many a cove and creek along the Silver Coast has its tale; a few of those are related here.

Reenactments of colonial-era and Civil War battles and events are popular at Brunswick's historic sites.

The Spanish Invasion

The Spanish flag of 1748

In the early autumn of 1748, three sloops appeared off Southport. Two were Spanish privateers, the third a prize taken in South Carolina waters. The largest of the three was the *Fortune*—130 tons with "10 six-pounders and 14 swivels, commanded by Vincent Lopez," according to an account published in an October 1748 issue of the *South Carolina Gazette*. What is now known as the Spanish invasion of Brunswick Town was related in vivid detail:[2]

It seems their design was to take the negroes that were at work on our fort; but being inform'd that few or none of them staid there on Sundays, and they were mostly at Brunswick, they obliged the pilots to carry them there, which was done without our discovering they were enemies, 'till they anchored before the town and had fired at some boats that retreated on finding their mistake. At the same time a large number of men, which they had landed 4 miles below the town, appeared within 100 yards of us. It is easy to imagine the confusion people must be in at such a surprise: In short, everybody (that was able) ran, with whatever they could first lay their hands on, whilst the Spaniards took possession of all the vessels in the harbour, *viz.* the ship *Nancy*, Capt. Barfill, the scow *Litchfield*, Capt. Wakefield, the brig *Diamond*, Capt. Bugnion,

A cannon raised from the Cape Fear River once graced the deck of the Spanish flagship.

the sloop, _____, Capt. Floddart, and several small craft. They also took two or three men belonging to the town, in boats.

The Spanish invaders had been guided into the river by the town's own pilots, welcomed as if they were guests! As the account goes, many citizens of Brunswick Town, after two days of being attacked by the invaders, grew weary of the shooting, and the plundering and destruction of property. They gathered to consider retaliation, even though they lacked arms and ammunition. The following day, on Tuesday, September the 6th, the account records:

We muster'd about 80 men, white and black, 22 of which were useless for want of arms. With this number Capt. [William] Dry marched towards the town, and the scouts sent out seeing nothing to disturb them, he march'd on until he got behind it, where a council of war was held, in consequence of which was that Lieut. Schinking Moore march'd into the town with 12 pick'd men, with which he in a few minutes surprised a number of the enemy that were rolling of[f] goods. Upon hearing the fire, Capt. Dry (concluding Lieut. Moore was engaged with the enemy) march'd his whole body in to his assistance. All the enemy in this part of

Spanish invaders, admitted to Brunswick Town by river pilots who were unaware they were the enemy, looted the town for two days before the settlers mounted a defense and captured them.

The painting of Christ, *Ecce Homo*, once hung on the wall of the Spanish ship destroyed during the raid on Brunswick Town but was given to St. James Church in Wilmington after the invaders' capture.

the town were either kill'd or taken, and our people pursuing their good fortune 'till they were saluted with a very hot fire from the commodore sloop's [*Fortune's*] great guns, which obliged them to be more on their guard, but however did not prevent their killing or taking all the stragglers.

The town being thus clear'd of the enemy, our men lay on their arms under cover of a high bank to prevent the landing [of] any more men, which was not attempted; but the commodore's sloop continued firing, when to our great amazement and (it may [be] believed) joy, she blew up; A terrible, tho' in our circumstances a pleasing sight.

The *Gazette* article continues with an account of an exchange of prisoners and the escape of the one remaining Spanish ship along with her South Carolina captive sloop. The invasion, which lasted from September 3 until September 8, 1748, was costly. But it was especially costly to the Spaniards. The account concludes:

We can get no positive account what number of men they brought in here, but by the number they carried out (between 70 and 80) and the great number buried and still to be buried, we judge they had about 260. How many our men killed is also very uncertain, since they were mostly shot in the water or thrown in afterwards: But we reckon this expedition has cost them (in kill'd and blown up) 140 men, among whom [were] Capt. Lopez and all his officers.

They have done us all the mischief they possibly could, for what they did not carry away they broke or cut to pieces. The negroes (whom they came to take) were of great service to us, and so exasperated, that they would have given no quarter had they not been stopt. We have not lost one Man, and had but two slightly wounded.

As with most buildings from old Burnswick Town, the foundation of the inn is all that remains today.

The Trial of the Snake

In these days of high-profile court cases and endless legal commentaries on television, it is amusing to consider a lesser known—but very real—criminal trial. The story concerns the escapades of Gen. Francis Marion, the famous "Swamp Fox" of Carolina legend, whose men were closely associated with Brunswick County. Marion's brother lived at the Boundary House in Calabash, and many of his maneuvers occurred along the Brunswick border.

The prisoner at the bar was a rattlesnake and the charge was murder. The place was about forty-five miles to the south and west of Myrtle Beach, South Carolina, near a place known as Gallivant's Ferry, during a time when the patriots and the British were engaged in frequent conflicts throughout the Carolinas. The trial, which took place in August, 1780, following one of Gen. Francis Marion's attacks on a British camp, was certainly a strange one.

Gen. Marion's men easily took the British soldiers, who had been previously drinking peach brandy. The Tories were killed or wounded, or escaped into the swamp. Marion's men, who had not eaten for days, did not pursue the enemy. They showed more interest in what the king's soldiers left behind: wild turkeys and pigs cooked over campfires, and plenty of peach brandy for all of Marion's men.

The next morning, the Americans, having consumed the food and wine through the night, began to search for the enemy who had escaped into the swamp. They came upon a body in British uniform. When the ensuing examination turned up no bullet wound, one soldier suggested that maybe the man had died of fright. Then another of the patriots spied a rattlesnake slithering under a bush.

When one soldier shouldered his gun, the man who found the snake jumped to the snake's defense. "Please don't kill him," he pleaded. "He might have a family waiting for him to come home to them." Marion's men were willing to spare the snake for the time being, but insisted that it be tried in a court-martial.

The snake's defender went to his horse and took a hair out of its tail, used it to make a noose on a small pole, and slipped it around the snake's neck. The man then carried the captured reptile over to the group. One of history's strangest judicial dramas shortly unfolded.

"You claim my client should be hanged for murder?" the soldier asked. "If this"—he held up the snake for all to see—"is a murderer, then we are too. He only killed one enemy soldier, but we have taken the lives of many. This was a case of war, not murder. He used his weapon like we do ours. This snake is not a foe, but an ally."

Immediately the court rose, lifted their mugs of brandy, and cried, "Not guilty"—and the snake was set free.

Stede Bonnet's version of the Jolly Roger flag featured the heart and dagger along with the skull and crossbones.

A Bit of Pirate Lore

IN THE EIGHTEENTH CENTURY THE Cape Fear region was a favorite meeting place for pirates, including the notorious Blackbeard and Mary Ann Blythe, the "Woman Buccaneer." The Brunswick Islands had its own day of pirates and plunder. Stede Bonnet (bon-NAY), sometimes known as the Gentleman Pirate, had a favorite hiding place for his ship near Smithville (now Southport). Bonnet's Creek is identified there by a marker on the ferry road heading north out of town.

Bonnet had been a wealthy plantation owner back in Barbados but left his well-heeled life for a more adventurous one as a pirate. A former major in the British army, Bonnet was exceptionally well educated for his time. He was born to wealth and privilege. He owned a sugar plantation on the island of Barbados and moved in the best circles there. He was also a landlubber with virtually no knowledge of the sea. It is hard to understand why he chose to become a pirate and associate himself with the crude, bloodthirsty dregs of the earth. (Some say he fled to the sea to escape a nagging wife.) Maj. Bonnet purchased a ship (an unusual act since pirates normally stole their vessels) turned to piracy and lived a life of plunder, murder and debauchery.

Bonnet was an amateur, however, and despite taking a few ships off the Carolinas, his crew was on the edge of mutiny when he chanced to meet up with the infamous English pirate Edward Teach. Blackbeard, as Teach was better known, made a terrible sight, with three braces of pistols, burning brands stuck behind his ears, and his black beard tied with a ribbon. Bonnet and Teach plundered together for a time— but Bonnet was swindled out of his share by the more experienced pirate before the pair split up. Bonnet continued sailing across the Caribbean and the Atlantic Oceans until one day in 1718 when his luck ran out.

The Gentleman Pirate and his motley crew had managed to upset British shipping to the point that in September 1718 two of His Majesty's ships, the *Henry* and the *Sea Nymph,* under the command of Col. William Rhett, were sent to put a stop to the raids. Rhett's ships caught up with Bonnet's *Royal James* (formerly the *Revenge*) at the mouth of the Cape Fear River.

In the ensuing "Battle of the Sandbars," during the thick of the battle the tide went out, grounding all three ships on sand bars beside present-day Battery Island, across from Southport. The immobilized ships continued to hurl cannonballs back and forth until the pirates finally gave up. The captured pirates were taken from Brunswick to Charles Town (Charleston, South Carolina), where fifteen of them were promptly hanged.

Stede Bonnet met his fate a year later—after having escaped for fourteen days and been recaptured—when he was led to the gallows in Charleston. As he went to his death, he held in his manacled hands a bouquet of flowers that a small girl had picked for him.

As a historical side note: Bonnet's onetime partner in crime met a similarly grim fate. A ship sent by the governor of Virginia at last caught up with Blackbeard and his cohorts on Ocracoke Island. A fierce battle ensued, and the pirate captain was overwhelmed. Teach was wounded twenty-five times before being decapitated by a swordsman.

His last words were, "Well done, lad!", spoken to the swordsman who had clumsily cut his prisoner's neck before delivering the final blow.

Near Beaufort Inlet, farther up the North Carolina coast, divers in 1996 came upon what appears to be the centuries-old wreck of Blackbeard's flagship, *Queen Anne's Revenge.*

Researchers do not know for certain, but officials at the North Carolina Department of Archives and History think that this may be her. The ship's fate had been the subject of conjecture for years. Found only a few yards off the coast in well-traveled waters, the wreck likely became visible after Hurricane Floyd disturbed the bottom of the inlet.

Recently the state has undertaken to cover the wreck again with dredged sand, to preserve it from further exposure and deterioration.

The Barefooted Felons Affair

JOHN DANIELL, A COLONIAL SHIP OWNER FROM Charleston, was in the business of transporting all manner of commerce between London and Carolina.

One warm day in 1717 as his ship neared Charleston, a pirate ship was spotted in the distance. Pirates had discovered that it was to their advantage to lurk just over the horizon from a busy port and wait for prey.

Quick calculations revealed to Mr. Daniell that the pirate ship, having the wind, would overtake his ship before it could reach safety. The necessity of evading a cruel fate mothered a clever idea. He ordered his crew to put their shoes on, a strange command in days when sailors commonly went barefoot, especially in warm weather. He then ordered them to quickly gather everything made of glass on his ship and smash it. The shards of glass were then spread all over the deck.

When the barefooted pirates overtook the vessel and came swinging aboard, they were greeted by a most unpleasant experience. As they danced about trying to avoid the glass, the would-be thieves found themselves at a great disadvantage in their pursuit of plunder.

Their distress was of such a serious degree that they were overcome by the well-shod crewmen of the merchant ship, and their own ill-gotten treasury came into the possession of Mr. Daniell and his crew. The pirates' misfortune became the fortune that enabled John Daniell to purchase a fine plantation on the Lockwood Folly River where the present-day town of Supply is located. Daniell had little knowledge of farming, but, as was common in those days, he hired an overseer to take charge, and subsequently became very prosperous, wealthy, and influential.

Daniell served as a justice of the peace in 1743, 1745, and 1750 and was appointed county road commissioner in 1745. His name appears on the list of men on duty at the Spanish Alarm of 1748 under Capt. John Sherard. John Daniell lived out his days on his plantation until his death in 1763.

Driven from the islands of the West Indies in the 1700s, pirates found the myriad inlets and creeks of the North Carolina coast an ideal haven.

Today the home of the commander of the Sunny Point Military Terminal occupies the site of old Fort Johnston.

The Old Fort

FROM ITS EARLIEST DAYS, BRUNSWICK TOWN WAS at risk of becoming caught up in the old rivalry between England and Spain.

In 1744 growing fear of Spanish attack caused the governor's council to meet in emergency session to plan for the defense of the Cape Fear area. After a nine-month search for the best location, a site was selected near the mouth of the Cape Fear River on the western side, at present-day Southport. The fortification would be named Fort Johnston in honor of the royal governor of North Carolina, Gabriel Johnston.

The Spanish did not wait for the fort to be finished before launching an attack.

A British soldier during the period of Fort Johnston's construction

The construction, begun in 1745, was not even half finished when the Spanish struck Brunswick Town in 1748. It would be another seven years before the fortifications were completed.

In February 1776 the British sloop of war *Diligence* was confronted by armed militia at Brunswick Town and denied permission to unload its cargo of tax stamps. The captain of the *Diligence*, fearing that Fort Johnston might fall into the hands of the rebelling militia, took it upon himself to have its cannons spiked, or rendered inoperable.

It has been rumored that Royal Governor Tryon was furious when he heard this and ordered Captain Lobb of the *Diligence* to restore the guns at once.

King George II had presented Fort Johnston with a gift of twenty-four

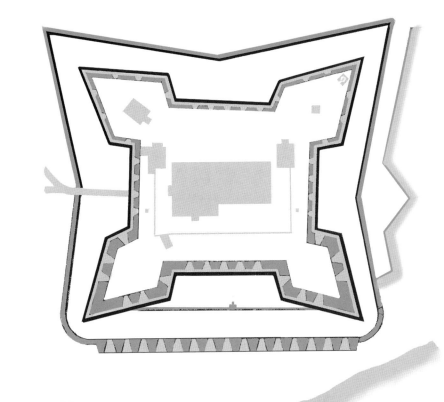

The colonial-era Fort Johnston was a refinement of the basic type of fortification used in the seventeenth and eighteenth centuries known as a star redoubt. The star-shaped design of the central complex allowed the defenders' guns to protect every point of the fort's perimeter.

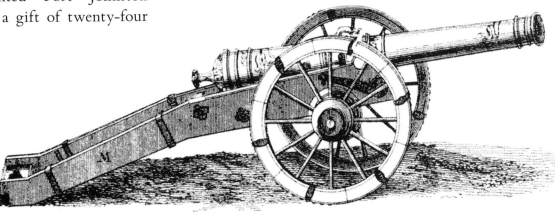

In 1776 the British left Fort Johnston and its twenty-four cannon in the charge of five soldiers.

cannons. It is therefore difficult to understand why in 1776 the fort had a complement of only five soldiers. How was such a small contingent of men to handle so many guns?

The last act for the once mighty bastion occurred when the last royal governor of North Carolina, Josiah Martin, fled from his palace in New Bern and took refuge in Fort Johnston. The final curtain came down on royal government in North Carolina and on Fort Johnston as well, when Governor Martin sailed away on HMS *Cruizer* in July 1775.

The patriots promptly demolished Fort Johnston—an act they later sorely regretted.

Josiah Martin, the last royal governor of North Carolina from 1734 to 1752

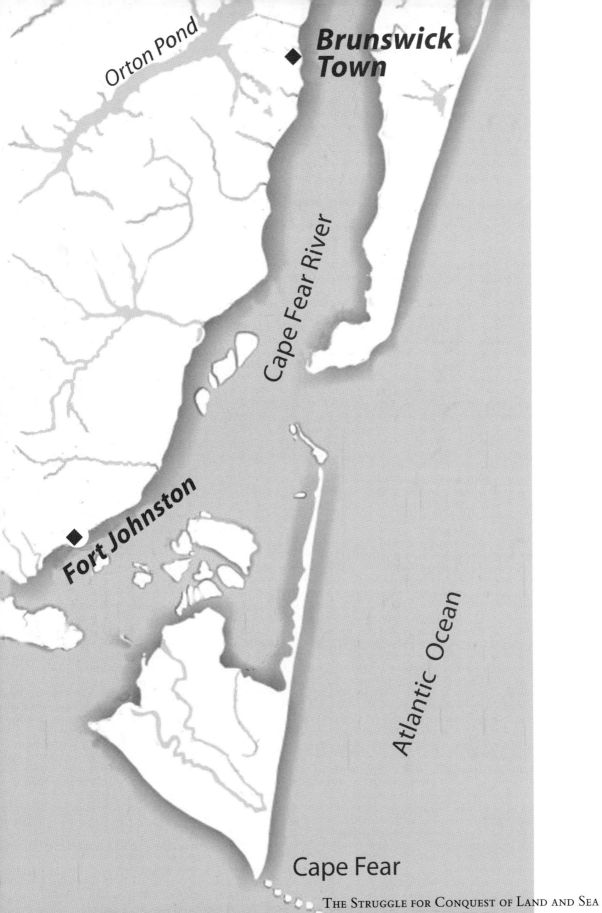

Orton Pond

◆ **Brunswick Town**

Cape Fear River

◆ **Fort Johnston**

Atlantic Ocean

Cape Fear

Fort Anderson and the River Forts

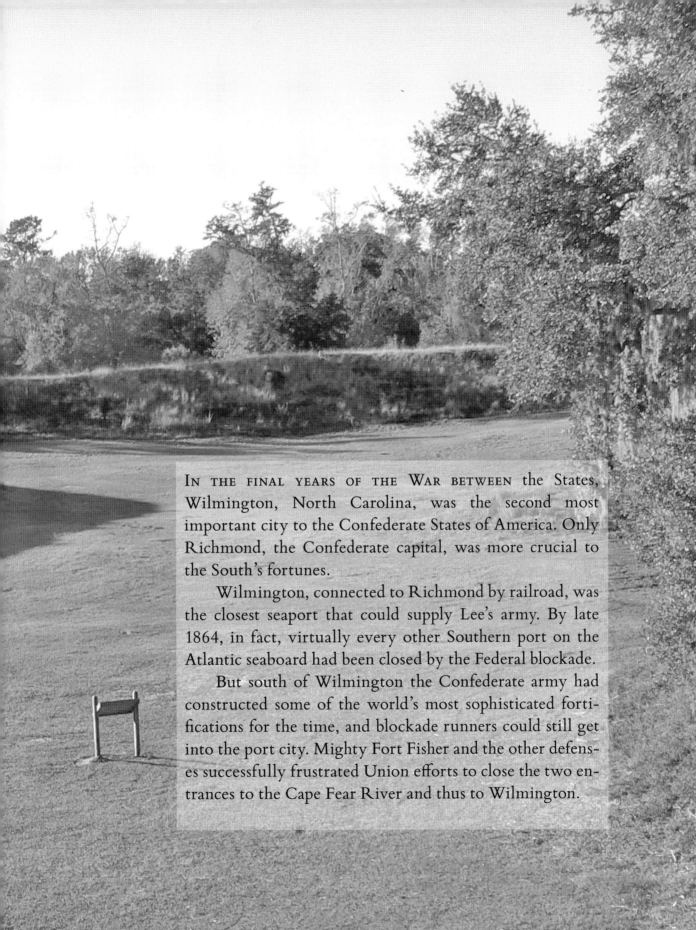

IN THE FINAL YEARS OF THE WAR BETWEEN the States, Wilmington, North Carolina, was the second most important city to the Confederate States of America. Only Richmond, the Confederate capital, was more crucial to the South's fortunes.

Wilmington, connected to Richmond by railroad, was the closest seaport that could supply Lee's army. By late 1864, in fact, virtually every other Southern port on the Atlantic seaboard had been closed by the Federal blockade.

But south of Wilmington the Confederate army had constructed some of the world's most sophisticated fortifications for the time, and blockade runners could still get into the port city. Mighty Fort Fisher and the other defenses successfully frustrated Union efforts to close the two entrances to the Cape Fear River and thus to Wilmington.

Col. William Lamb briefly commanded Fort Anderson before taking over the defense of Fort Fisher, the main Confederate bastion protecting Wilmington.

Next in importance to Fort Fisher among the river forts guarding Wilmington stood Fort Anderson. Constructed in 1862 as Fort St. Philip on the site of what had once been Brunswick Town, the fort was originally named after the town's St. Philip's Church and parish.

By the time the fort was constructed, the town had been reclaimed by dense forest. The old town had stood on a high bluff overlooking the wide river. It was an excellent site for a fort. Orton Pond, to the rear of the site, provided an additional dividend by thwarting potential land assaults.

Maj. Thomas Rowland, a gifted engineer and a West Point graduate, began vigorous construction of the fort in 1862. When Maj. Rowland was transferred out of the Cape Fear District he was succeeded by another energetic officer with a zeal for engineering, William Lamb. Lamb had been serving under Maj. Rowland and went on to command Fort Fisher after briefly commanding Fort St. Philip.

The names of all the fortifications in the Cape Fear District were changed to commemorate the Confederate dead of North Carolina, and Fort St. Philip was rechristened Fort Anderson (likely named in honor of Brig. Gen. George Burgwyn Anderson, killed in 1862 at the Battle of Sharpsburg). Anderson was a direct ancestor of John Burgwin, whose home was used by Gen. Cornwallis as his headquarters during the Revolutionary War occupation of Wilmington.

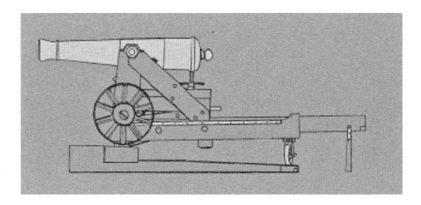

A cannon of the type used in Confederate coastal fortifications.

Fort Anderson is likely named for Brig. Gen. George Burgwyn Anderson, killed at Sharpsburg in 1862.

After the Union's disastrous attempt to take Fort Fisher in December 1864, a second massive attempt was undertaken in January 1865. The second assault was all-out. The Union navy unleashed the largest bombardment in history up to that time, and the federal army landed an overwhelming number of soldiers to assault Fort Fisher from the land.

Col. Lamb and his men made a truly heroic defense but to no avail. The young colonel was badly wounded and the fort fell.

The garrisons of forts Holmes, Campbell, Pender and Caswell were withdrawn to reinforce Fort Anderson, whose turn would be next.

By January 19, 1865, Federals controlled everything up to Battery Lamb, only four miles from Fort Anderson but they waited to amass overwhelming force before attacking.

By February 1865 the Confederates had managed to assemble about 2,300 men to defend Fort Anderson. This would be a pitiful force, however, compared to the numbers against them.

When word reached the commander of the Cape Fear District, Gen. Hoke, that Fort Anderson was about to be invaded from the rear and cut off from Wilmington, he ordered the fort evacuated to save its garrison. The defenders of the fort quietly slipped out on the night of February 18 and marched up the road to Town Creek, where they took up new positions to further delay the fall of Wilmington.

With the dawn, the Union tide broke over the empty fort and was greeted by shells from their own ships in the river. The last shots fired at Fort Anderson were blue on blue! The Union navy was fighting against the Union army.

The numerous forts that guarded the mouth of the Cape Fear River in the Civil War era assured that the port of Wilmington remained open until the last months of the war.

An Ironclad Proposal

THE USS *NORTH CAROLINA*, ONE OF the most powerful battleships of World War II, rests today on the northeastern border of Brunswick County. The vessel was the most decorated warship of its era, earning fifteen battle stars. A few years after it was decommissioned following the war's end, North Carolinians mounted a campaign to bring the ship home to a permanent site as a museum and memorial. A small slice of Brunswick County land was later transferred to the Battleship property to enlarge the memorial site.

A few miles to the south, sleeping on the bottom of the Cape Fear River, lies a similarly named vessel from an earlier war—the CSS *North Carolina*. The original *North Carolina* sank there in 1867 after losing a destructive battle with toreutic marine worms. The victorious worms have left only the hull's wooden skeleton for archaeologists to excavate. The rest of the once-mighty ironclad has fallen victim to the voracious appetite of the greedy little worms.

Surviving ironclads are very rare, and the CSS *North Carolina* is considered by the experts working in conjunction with Army Corps of Engineers to be an important piece of history. The wreck of the CSS *North Carolina* lies underwater just to the west of Battery Island at Southport's waterfront. But her name lives on in the illustrious namesake, the great "Showboat" permanently berthed upriver.

The CSS North Carolina, a Civil War ironclad

Blockade runners, sleek and fast, were designed to outrun Union warships.

Blockade Runners

DURING THE WAR BETWEEN THE States, the Confederate States of America possessed only a very small navy. The Confederate force could not hope to drive off the powerful blockading squadrons of the United States Navy, which would have rapidly brought the Confederate armies to their knees for lack of arms and ammunition. The South was rich in agriculture but extremely poor in manufacture.

Since necessity is the mother of invention, the rebels presented a solution: the blockade runners. They were very fast and very sleek ships, some possessing folding smokestacks and camouflage paint. These ships were designed to outrun the Union warships and to sneak through the blockade on foggy or stormy nights.

The area from the mouth of the Cape Fear River down to Sunset Beach and Tubbs Inlet saw a good deal of naval action between blockade runners of the Confederacy and gunboats of the Union Navy.

On September 24, 1863, the blockade runner *Elizabeth* was sunk by gunfire from a Union gunboat directly off Holden Beach. On January 4, the blockade runner *Bendigo* tried to run the warship gauntlet of the *North* and was sunk about two miles off Lockwood Folly Inlet. The blockade runner *Vesta* was sunk off Tubbs Inlet on January 10, 1864, fleeing from a gunboat while trying to enter the inlet.

During the Civil War, Tubbs Inlet was a major outlet into the Atlantic. It has since shoaled over and can be navigated only by small boats at high tide.

A Union gunboat, the *Iron Age*, and a blockade runner, the *Ranger*, were both sunk in an encounter off Lockwood Folly on January 11, 1864.

Storms and shifting sands have destroyed most of the sunken vessels, but the *Vesta's* iron works were visible for many years directly off the mouth of Tubbs Inlet at Sunset Beach. In the 1960s it could still be seen through the slats of the Sunset Beach pier. Several times each year when the ocean is affected by unusually high and low tides, the wooden keel of the blockade runner *Ranger* is exposed at low tide, off Holden Beach.

The sands of Brunswick's beaches have hidden many secrets over the ages.

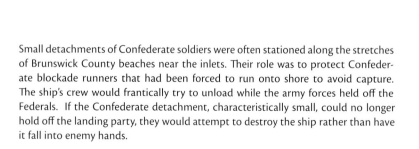

Small detachments of Confederate soldiers were often stationed along the stretches of Brunswick County beaches near the inlets. Their role was to protect Confederate blockade runners that had been forced to run onto shore to avoid capture. The ship's crew would frantically try to unload while the army forces held off the Federals. If the Confederate detachment, characteristically small, could no longer hold off the landing party, they would attempt to destroy the ship rather than have it fall into enemy hands.

A Strange Bird on the Beach

ONE DAY IN THE SPRING OF 2000, Ocean Isle Beach's building inspector, Larry Cook, discovered a corroded piece of history and legend that had emerged from the sands of the island's east end just a few blocks west of The Winds resort. What he found were the remains of a World War II Navy fighter temporarily exposed by the waves and shifting sands along the beach.

"I knew it was there from folklore," Mr. Cook said. "It was rumored to have been there—and sure enough she came up."

The wreck of the propeller-driven plane had been spotted intermittently over the years, but it had never surfaced long enough to attract the attention that surrounded it that week.

"The previous building inspector told me it was there," Cook said. "He'd heard some kids had dug down five feet and found a wing. Yesterday we found a machine gun. It wasn't even low tide. People were just digging around it like a treasure hunt."

The area was roped off and an ordnance disposal team from Pope Air Force Base was sent to check for any remaining live ammunition. None was found.

The plane was first thought to be an F-6F Hellcat but was later identified as an Army Air Corps P-47D Thunderbolt after further excavation and inspection exposed the plane's numbers on the wings.

Air Corps flight records show that Lt. Robert Boyd, based during the war at Bluethenthal Field, now the Wilmington airport, went down on June 29, 1944, at 1615 hours when he failed to switch to his auxiliary fuels tanks and literally ran out of gas. Lt. Boyd landed on the beach with his wheels in the up position but

was not injured in the crash, although he probably suffered a bruised ego when his fellow fliers heard about the incident.

While the plane's recent emergence has drawn crowds of curious onlookers to the beach, the rediscovery has also provided several longtime residents, who had seen parts of it intermittently exposed over the years, a chance to view the whole thing.

Eldridge Stanley of the Brick Landing area first spotted the plane back in 1944 as an eleven-year-old, he said, when the barrel-shaped plane plunged out of the sky, skipped across the ocean, and skidded onto the then uninhabited beach.

"It kicked up a lot of spray because that propeller was still turning when it hit the waterway," Mr. Stanley said.

He recalled it was one of two military aircraft that crashed onto the beach as he and his brother stood outside their grandfather's fishing shack on a clear, late summer morning.

"There was always two," said Mr. Stanley, who retired from the Army Corps of Engineers after years of recovering downed jets from Pamlico Sound. "They patrolled the beach every day. It got to be where we would watch for them."

Some days the pilots would fly low enough as they patrolled to wave at the two boys. Mr. Stanley speculates that the planes were possibly searching for German submarines known to prowl the Eastern seaboard during the war.

"All of a sudden this one veered off," he said. "We thought it was going to land on the beach strand. . . . You know how a rock skips? Well, that's just the way she skipped."

The other plane crashed only minutes later near Shallotte Inlet—and Mr. Stanley, who was fishing on Ocean Isle Beach at the time, witnessed both crashes. The second aircraft was recovered by a barge

A U.S. Army Air Corps P-47D Thunderbolt, one of the fastest and most effective fighter planes of World War II sent up from the Charleston Naval Shipyard in South Carolina, he said. The first, however, was not as easy to recover and was left where it went down. Due to the strange coincidence of the dual crashes, Mr. Stanley said, rumor was that sabotage was involved—but it remained a matter of local speculation.

Both pilots emerged from their wrecks unscathed. Mr. Stanley remembers that the men met back at his grandfather's fishing shack to wait for the Coast Guard to pick them up.

When the wreck reemerged, Ocean Isle Beach town manager Greg Taylor went through weeks of phone calls and e-mails back and forth from Army and Air Force contacts to determine who had salvage rights to the plane. It was finally decided that the town had ownership—but had nowhere to keep it safe and preserved. In the end the town donated the remains of the plane to the Carolina History of Aviation Museum in Charlotte, North Carolina, where it was transported for preservation.

Records indicate that more than 15,000 P-47D Thunderbolts were built. Only 60 of the aircraft are still intact, with about a dozen of those in condition to be flown—though not the one that met its untimely demise decades ago on Ocean Isle Beach.

Coast Guard Cavalry

A LONE RIDER IS SILHOUETTED AGAINST a seemingly endless expanse of sand. His gaze is on the distant horizon; in his saddlebags he carries binoculars, water, and a few other essentials. A .45 caliber submachine gun hangs in a leather scabbard on his horse's side and he carries a .38 caliber revolver in the holster on his belt.

Lawrence of Arabia? No, this man is Herman Love, the year is 1943, and the place is Hale's Beach—known today as the lively resort island of Ocean Isle Beach.

Mr. Love, twenty-two years old at the time, was a member of the U.S. Coast Guard Mounted Beach Patrol. He was part of a detachment of approximately twenty men whose mission was to ride along the beach and watch for spies, downed planes, blackout violations, signs of enemy invasion, or any other suspicious activity. On the remote barrier islands of North Carolina, where there were no roads, the easiest way to patrol was on horseback.

At the time, during the battles of the North Atlantic at the height of World War II, German submarines were routinely sinking merchant ships off of the East Coast of the United States. Mr. Love's detachment, and many more stationed elsewhere, watched the coastline twenty-four hours a day, 365 days a year.

At Hale's Beach their base, consisting of barracks, a stable, and a dock on the north shore of the island, provided the only structures on the island. The men and their horses were the only inhabitants besides the seabirds and other wildlife.

When Mr. Love left his home in Mokane, Missouri, to enlist in the Coast Guard, he had no idea where he would be stationed. It must have been quite an adventure—not to mention quite a shock—to find himself in this beautiful but desolate location at a time when the only paved roads in Brunswick County were Highway 17 (then just two lanes), and the roads to Whiteville and Southport. There wasn't any electricity in the county either.

"We never did catch any spies," Mr. Love said in an interview a few years back. "But we had a few planes crash. They were using the island for gunnery practice. Some pilots were killed on Holden Beach. The ones on Ocean Isle got out all right. It was our job to watch over the planes until some one came to get them. They didn't want the gun sights falling into enemy hands."

The natural beauty and serenity of the area must have taken hold on Mr. Love, because after the war he settled here and married a local girl.

A lone mounted patrol scans the beach for German vessels during World War II.

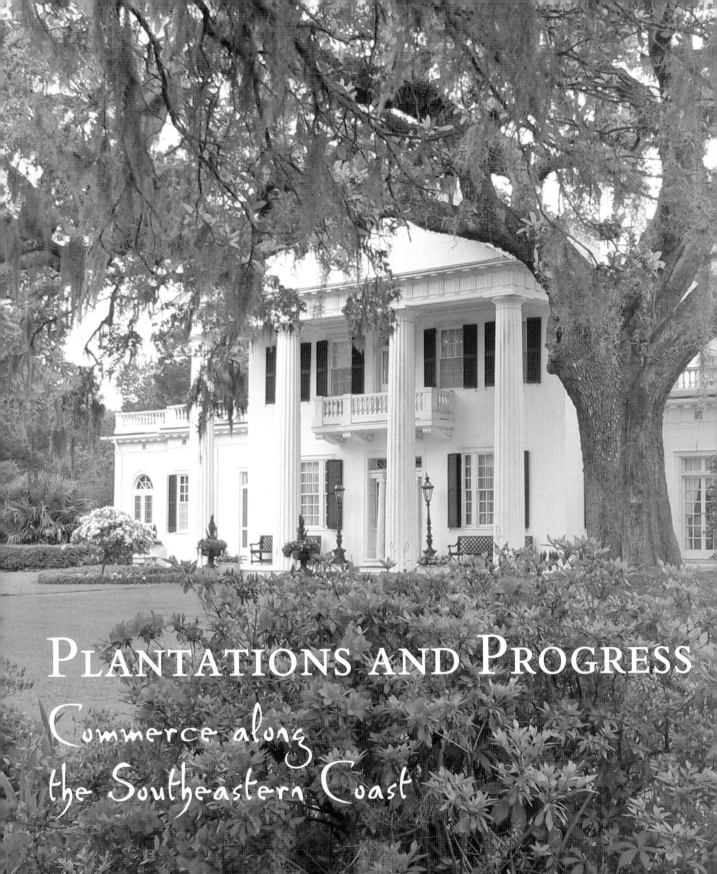

PLANTATIONS AND PROGRESS

Commerce along
the Southeastern Coast

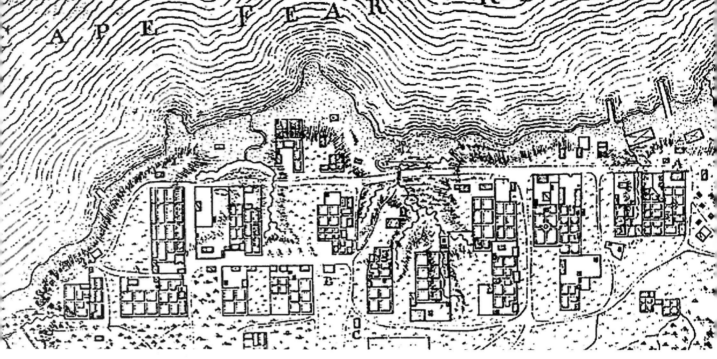

Brunswick Town was laid out in 1725 by Roger Moore on the west bank of the Cape Fear River. OVERLEAF: The magnificent home at Orton Plantation was expanded and renovated in the early 1900s by the Sprunt family, current owners of the vast estate.

Old Brunswick

THE LITTLE TOWN CALLED BRUNSWICK was never very large, not much larger than a village, really. Yet during the brief five decades it flourished, the town played a very important role in the formation of the United States.

During little Brunswick's heyday, it was North Carolina's main seaport and served as the provincial capital. It was the largest supplier of naval stores for the ships of the mighty British Empire, and it exported rice and indigo to the world.

At the time just after the American Revolution a number of leaders of the young republic called Brunswick Town home—more than might be expected in a relatively small and isolated place.

Gen. Robert Howe, commander of the fortress of West Point and president of the court-martial that tried Benedict Arnold, was born in Brunswick in 1734; he was North Carolina's highest-ranking officer during the Revolution.

Col. Benjamin Smith, George Washington's aide-de-camp and later governor of North Carolina, was born in Brunswick County.

Cornelius Harnett, a member of the Continental Congress and signer of the Declaration of Independence, was born in Chowan County but came to Brunswick to farm.

Alfred Moore, attorney general of North Carolina and later a justice of the first

The younger Maurice Moore (a son of Maurice Moore, one of the first settlers in the Cape Fear region) was born in Brunswick County in 1735. Moore was one of the three colonial judges of North Carolina when he joined the patriot cause at the beginning of the American Revolution. He was a member of the committee of the provincial House of Burgesses in 1775-1776 that drew up a protest to the people of Great Britain on the wrongs of the American colonies. He also played a major part in forming the state constitution. He died at the same hour as his brother James in Wilmington on January 15, 1777.

Colonial governor Arthur Dobbs, born in Ireland in 1784, served as a member of the Irish parliament before becoming the governor of North Carolina in November 1754. He remained in office until 1765, though continued disputes with the legislature marked his administration. The representatives of the people refused to provide for government expenses when the governor insisted upon unpopular measures on behalf of the British government. Governor Dobbs died at Town Creek in Brunswick County on March 28, 1765.

Alfred Moore was born in Brunswick County May 25, 1755. Educated in Boston, he was only twenty years old when he was admitted to the bar. In 1775 he gave up his profession to become a captain in the 1st North Carolina Regiment, of which his uncle James Moore was colonel. After fighting in the Revolutionary battles of Charleston and Fort Moultrie he raised a troop of volunteers. He was elected North Carolina attorney general in 1792 and in 1799 was appointed an associate justice of the U.S. Supreme Court by the president. In 1805 he resigned his position because of ill health, and he died five years later.

Interior of Old St. Philip's Church, Brunswick Town's only remaining standing building.

United States Supreme Court, was born at Brunswick, the son of Col. Maurice Moore. The list goes on—the little town made a contribution to the founding of the United States far out of proportion to its size.

Brunswick Town was founded by Roger Moore, a younger brother of Col. Maurice Moore, who had been granted a vast amount of land on the Cape Fear River in 1725. The Moores and their followers had all come from the Caribbean island of Barbados via Charleston in South Carolina.

Roger Moore initially purchased a site from his brother near Orton, his brother's plantation that he would also eventually acquire. He laid out lots on the site and began selling them. A town was soon underway. The little town made an excellent port, situated on a high bluff where the Cape Fear River was about a mile wide and deep enough for large vessels to enter.

As plantations sprang up along the river and people began to settle the interior, the merchants of Brunswick began shipping products to the world. Brunswick even had a few ship owners. Arthur Dobbs, the royal governor in charge of North Carolina, directed the colony's affairs from Russellborough, a large, unfinished house on the outskirts of Brunswick, beginning in 1758.

He was succeeded there by Gov. William Tryon, who began his tenure in office at Brunswick in 1764 but would later move to New Bern.

When the relative tranquility of little Brunswick was abruptly shattered in 1748 by the aborted Spanish raid, the citizens realized the vulnerability of their town to attack. They began to have other doubts. Despite their courageousness in opposing the Stamp Act in 1765 and their patriotic decision to outfit and send a ship to aid their fellow colonists in Boston after the famous Tea Party of 1773, it was not lost on the people of Brunswick Town that other North Carolina coastal cities were beginning to outstrip them in growth and promi-nence. In 1770 Governor Tryon decided to move the governor's residence—and thus the seat of the colonial government—back to New Bern, because of its more central location. The citizens of Brunswick felt the loss keenly.

Wilmington, twenty miles upriver, had become a thriving rival to its counter-part on the west bank of the river even before Gen. Sir Henry Clinton and his Brit-ish force descended on Brunswick in 1777 and destroyed a large part of the town.

For many, the British raid and de-struction was the last straw. They felt that Wilmington offered more safety, and they moved. The town was utterly deserted.

All that remains of Russellborough, the home of two of North Carolina's early governors and the site of much history.

By the time the Confederate forces decided to build a fort at the site, nearly eighty years later, the forests had reclaimed the ruins. Only the tabby walls of old St. Philip's Church still stood, as they still do today. St. Philip's had once been the grandest church in the colony.

From 1855 until 1862 the site of old Brunswick was again abuzz with activity, this time for purposes of war. But then, once again, a big sleep of another hundred years ensued. The dense forests once more covered over the forgotten site.

In 1954 the old Brunswick Town was rediscovered by researchers. When the state realized what a historic treasure they had, archeological excavations were undertaken.

Today the State of North Carolina maintains a fine little museum on the site, accessible via NC 133, the River Road between Southport and Wilmington, and you can walk down the streets of long ago and visit the remains of Fort Anderson. It is all free of charge and well worth a visit.

OPPOSITE: The ordinary Brunswick family of the colonial period wore homemade clothes of locally woven fabrics. Boys and girls alike often wore dresses until seven or eight years of age, as trousers were the most difficult garment to sew and dresses made it easier to change the child's clothes. Mothers had a lot to do. Boys' dresses were unadorned, while girls' dresses were trimmed with lace or other frills. RIGHT: In the modest houses of old Brunswick Town, an open hearth provided heat for warmth and cooking. ABOVE: The excavated foundation of a Brunswick Town house, where archaeological study began in earnest in the 1950s. BELOW: A reconstruction of the Neth Moore house at Brunswick Town.

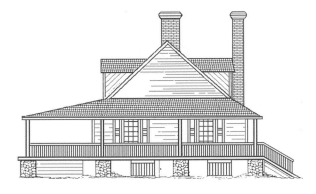

The Old Post Road

THE HIGHWAY THAT TODAY WINDS THROUGH North and South Carolina was known in colonial times as the King's Highway, in response to the wish of King Charles II in 1673 to establish communication among all the North American colonies. The old road was the chief means of land travel from Savannah, Georgia, through Charleston, South Carolina, and on to Boston, Massachusetts, beginning in the mid-1700s. At that time, Charleston was the wealthiest city in the colonies and Boston was the most northerly city of consequence.

Few people realize that this same road ran right through what is now Ocean Isle Beach. In fact, this is about the only place in its long route where it came so close to the ocean. The local people called it "The Old Stage Road," and you could traverse several miles of it as late as the mid-1970s when it came through the present site of a restaurant, on the Ocean Isle Causeway, and crossed Route 179 just south of the junction of Route 179 and Route 904 at Seaside.

This historic road was then only a sandy lane, about the width of a golf cart path. In fact, the cart path along the tenth fairway on the Maples Course at Sea Trail Plantation follows a portion of the old road. (Sea Trail took its name from the road, and the developers have named a section of homes The Royal Poste Villas.)

The old road played a part in the history of our country because of the armies and great leaders who marched and rode along it. George Washington followed the road on his southern tour in 1791, stopping at the home of William Gause, at Gause Landing, less than a mile west of the entrance to present-day Ocean Isle Beach.

Gause Landing has not received much note of its historical significance, but it was once a thriving place in an otherwise desolate area. In the journal of his southern tour (the text of which is available at the Library of Congress's website of the George Washington Papers), Washington wrote in the entry for Wednesday, April 27, 1791: "Breakfasted at Willm. Gause's a little out of the direct Road 14 Miles—crossed the boundary line between No. & South Carolina abt. half after 12 oclock which is 10 miles from Gauses."[3]

Another well-known figure also visited Gause Landing around that time. Methodist bishop Francis Asbury noted several visits there in his diary. On February 7, 1799, he wrote: "Came to 'father' William Gause's where I preached on Friday the 8th . . . paid a visit to the sea, and saw the breakers—awfully tremendous sight and sound."[4]

The Gause family had come to Brunswick County from Horry County, South Carolina prior to the Revolutionary War. William Sr. built a fine house beneath giant oak trees on a bluff overlooking a saltwater creek, now a part of the Intracoastal Waterway. From there he loaded crops for shipment and received cargo from overseas. Nearby was a landing where bricks were unloaded from England to build his manor house (said to be the origin of today's Brick Landing residential community). How different things must have been when Washington rode down that sandy wilderness path to pay a visit to the Gause family.

The Gause house is long gone, but the landing road, lined with ancient live oaks festooned with Spanish Moss, is still there. Visitors can imagine the early days of the American republic, when the first president of the new nation traveled these very lanes and highways.

In the eighteenth century prestigious families prospered on plantations and estates in southern Brunswick County, some from lands in South Carolina.

The site of the old boundary house in Calabash is obscured by woods today; in earlier times the house marked the state boundary between North and South Carolina.

The Old House on the Boundary

ACCORDING TO HIS 1773 JOURNAL, ITINERANT minister Joseph Pilmoor (who had preached the first Methodist sermon in North Carolina in 1772), stopped to eat at the "Boundary House" and indicated that this structure stood exactly on the line between the two Carolinas.

He stated that the Boundary House had been built by twenty-four gentlemen—twelve from each province—as a meeting place. He further noted that the accommodations were extremely good.

The site chosen was a good one; it sits on a rise only a few hundred feet from the Calabash River near Little

Gen. Benjamin Smith of North Carolina was injured in an 1805 duel with Capt. Maurice Moore at the Boundary House.

River Inlet. It would have been the most convenient place to meet in the 1700s, when most travel was by boat. The site also enjoys a magnificent view.

When the province of Carolina was divided into North and South Carolina in 1712, the boundary between the two provinces was the Cape Fear River. All the land which became Brunswick County was in South Carolina.

In November 1729, the North Carolina General Assembly created New Hanover County and they moved the boundary southeast to Little River Inlet. In 1735 the present boundary was officially established, and the Boundary House was probably built a short time afterward.

Over the years the Boundary House served as a meeting place, a place to hold religious services, a "public house" or tavern, and a place of residence.

On May 9, 1775, a courier from Brunswick Town arrived there, bearing the news of the Battle of Lexington. Justice of the Peace Isaac Marion, an older brother of "Swamp Fox" Francis Marion, was living at the Boundary House. He rushed the message to the Committee of Safety at Little River and other committees southward to Charleston and Savannah.

A granite boundary marks the state line—and the site of the Boundary House—today.

In 1776 The Boundary House briefly paid host to General Nash and his army of nine thousand Continental soldiers who encamped around the building while on the march from Wilmington to Charleston.

It is also sometimes rumored that George Washington slept at the Boundary House on his southern tour in 1791. Though it is not known for certain, since the Boundary House was on his route it's likely he at least stopped there.

The Boundary House was considered an ideal place to fight duels. North Carolina law forbade dueling, so it was an easy matter to just step over the line if North Carolina officers arrived to break up an illegal fight.

On June 28, 1805, Gen. Benjamin Smith and Capt. Maurice Moore held a duel at the boundary house. Both men fired and missed.[5] They both took one pace forward

and fired again. General Smith fell to the ground with a bullet in his chest. He recovered—going on to fight more duels and to become governor of North Carolina.

An old North Carolina law would not allow the body of a debtor to be released for burial until the debt was paid, and according to a story, when Gen. Smith later died in debt, his family secretly buried the body. Years later, when family members attempted to locate the body, they were unable to positively identify it. But a local woman told them that that the bullet taken at the Boundary House had never been removed. Using a sifter to sort through the remains, she found the bullet that identified the general.

By the time of the Civil War, the Boundary House was in ruin (a mapping error refers to "Old Boundary House Chimney"). The line was surveyed again in 1928, and the surveyors located the brick used in the house's chimney and piers.[6] Today only a small, slender stone monument stands in the tall grass to mark the site of this house that witnessed so much history.

Most men of the American Revolutionary War militia, lacking uniforms or military-issue weapons, wore their everyday clothing and were armed with their own hunting rifles.

The gates of Orton Plantation, one of the grandest of the old rice plantations, stand open today to invite visitors. Orton was spared the torch of the Union Army in the Civil War because it was used as a hospital.

Plantations of Bygone Days

THE GREAT PLANTATIONS OF THE CAPE FEAR River and Brunswick County are almost all gone now; only a few remain intact. At one time the large estates lined the Cape Fear River, and almost every stream that could float a vessel large enough to carry commerce had a beautiful home on its banks. A boat landing was an absolute necessity—before the railroad, it cost as much to transport a wagonload of goods thirty miles overland as it cost to transport it to Europe by water.

LEFT: The indigo plant yielded a rich blue dye in great demand for fabrics at home and in Europe. OPPOSITE: When prices for American indigo fell due to east Indian competition in the late eighteenth century, southerners turned to rice as a cash crop.

In this region the great houses were surrounded by vast fields of rice, peanuts, or cotton. Some plantations earned handsome sums from turpentine, tar, and other naval stores from the pine forests as well. The impact of the plantations on the lives of the owners and their families, the slaves who tended the houses and fields, and the local and regional economy cannot be overestimated. As historian Kenneth Stampp puts it,

Depending upon the labor of slaves who constituted the great majority of the American black population, the plantations were both homes and business enterprises for a white, southern elite. They were the largest, the most commercialized, and on the whole, the most efficient and specialized agricultural enterprises of their day, producing the bulk of the South's staple crops . . . Their proprietors were entrepreneurs who aspired to and sometimes, after a generation or two, achieved the status of a cultivated landed aristocracy. Many distinguished themselves not only in agriculture but in the professions, in the military, in government service, and in scientific and cultural endeavors.[7]

Before the American Revolution, indigo, the source of a blue dye, was a valuable crop in the Lower Cape Fear. It had been subsidized by the British government as a counterweight against indigo grown in French colonies. The young daughter of a Carolina plantation owner had brought indigo plants from a Caribbean island and started an indigo boom.

The cultivation of rice in low-lying coastal areas was a labor-intensive endeavor. Hoeing (above) was done in the hot summer months by large numbers of African slaves. An intricate series of ditches, dikes, and gates (opposite, top) controlled flooding of the fields. When the rice was harvested, slaves winnowed it by hand to separate the valuable grain (opposite, below).

The Cape Fear marked the northern limit of the rice empire, but it was here that some of the finest rice was grown. Orton Plantation, whose main house still stands in all its resplendence, grew seed rice for other plantations further south. Orton was spared from the Union Army torch because it was used as a hospital. The gardens at Orton are open to the public and are especially popular as a tourist spot during the spring. The house, which is still used on occasion by the owners, the Sprunt family, and is not open to the public, but the grounds alone provide a sense of what the Cape Fear landscape was like in centuries past. If you want to see a real "Gone with the Wind" plantation house, this is it. The house and gardens have been used as the location of several major films.

For a fine example of a restored working plantation, visitors can travel across the river and north of Wilmington on Highway 17 to Poplar Grove. The house and outbuildings of this former peanut plantation are open to the public, and special programs are frequently scheduled. Several Brunswick communities of today, such as Belville and Leland, are named for earlier plantations.

Rice was separated from the hull in winnowing barns raised on piers, above the threat of flood and vermin.

The Gause plantation, which stood just across the Intracoastal Waterway from Ocean Isle in southern Brunswick County, had the honor of housing George Washington overnight. President Washington visited the Gause family in 1791 on his way overland to Savannah via the King's Highway.

Other plantations have survived, but their owners seek seclusion and their estates are not open to the public.

Today the rice for southern tables is grown in California and Texas, and cotton fields, for the most part, are a faded memory in this area. Tobacco, a comparative newcomer to Brunswick County, is grown on small farms and became the region's primary cash crop throughout most of the twentieth century.

These days a new crop is making big inroads, occupying many acres of former plantation land: Coastal Bermuda grass—vast fairways of it!

Salt of the Earth

IN THE ERA OF MODERN REFRIGERATION of food, it is difficult to fully appreciate the vital part that salt played in the daily lives of the American population. Salt—plain old sodium chloride—was crucial for food preservation and for the health of humans and livestock.

The history of the salt industry in the Brunswick County area begins with William Hilton's exploration in 1662, when local Indians brought the Englishman a gift of salt, and lasted until the end of the Civil War in 1865.

During revolutionary days, salt was considered by the Continental Congress to be as essential as arms and ammunition to the survival of the emerging nation. Without salt, it would have required but little force to subdue and starve the province of North Carolina and the other colonies.

Because the region's ability to import the commodity was limited during wartime, and it did not naturally occur in deposits for mining, salt had to be produced locally in salt works. The coast of Brunswick and North Carolina came alive with men extracting salt by evaporating sea water.

When the South was blockaded during the Civil War, salt imports were again restricted. Salt was manufactured to supply the demand. By 1863 salt production had become an $8 million business with a vast State Salt Works and more than a hundred private works in the Lower Cape Fear area.

Most of the able-bodied white men had gone off to serve in the Confederate forces when the war temporarily disrupted both the production of naval stores and lumber. Salt was so important to the Confederacy that, for a period of time, it exempted commercial salt workers from serving in the military. As a consequence, however, Union troops considered salt workers as soldiers, subject to capture or worse!

Salt quickly rose in price during the war as entrepreneurs flocked to the coast to set up crude seawater evaporators. The salt-works operators knew that if they were spotted they would be shelled or attacked by marines sent ashore in small armed boats. The large salt works were usually guarded by Confederate troops stationed nearby.

Aside from blockade running and attacks on the river forts, most of the military action in Brunswick County involved the defense or destruction of the salt works. With the end of the war in 1865, salt could once again be produced more economically elsewhere, and large-scale salt manufacture in Brunswick County came to an end.

The *George Slover* was one of the rivergoing schooners still plying the waters between Shallotte and Wilmington in the early twentieth century.

Before the Road

As the town of Shallotte geared up for its centennial celebration in 1999, local "old-timer" Elwood Cheers recalled his childhood memories of the area for a newspaper article. He spoke of the days before they built "the road" (US Highway 17) in the late 1930s. Before that time, the inhabitants of coastal Brunswick County relied on sailing schooners for food staples and medicines.

Back before "the road," a thirty-mile trip to Wilmington to pick up supplies could take up to three days due to the poor traveling conditions.

At the turn of the century schooners with names like the *George Slover* and the *Addie May* plied their way up and down the Shallotte River, taking on and discharging their cargo at the thriving port of Wilmington and at the docks of the river's namesake at Shallotte.

"As a youngster," said Mr. Cheers, "I remember seeing the boats moored at a slip in the river or at a dock. At that time they were just a part of the riverside scenery, and hardly anyone had in mind the significance of the part that they played in the birth of our fledgling community."

Other major mooring points included Brick Landing, where they brought in—you guessed it—bricks.

The Atlantic Intracoastal Waterway provides safe passage for commercial and recreational vessels along 1,200 miles of the Eastern seaboard.

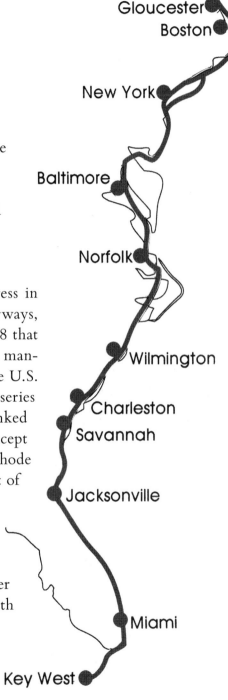

The Inland Waterway

The Atlantic Intracoastal Waterway winds down the East Coast of the United States for 1,200 miles, serving ports from Boston to Key West. This great sheltered artery was built between 1793 and 1939 by private canal companies and the U.S. Army Corps of Engineers; the section through North Carolina was built between 1914 and 1934.

An "inland waterway" was authorized by Congress in 1919 and utilized many existing canals and natural waterways, but it was not until the Rivers and Harbors Act of 1938 that the Atlantic Intracoastal Waterway was authorized and mandated by the government. It is maintained today by the U.S. Army Corps of Engineers. The waterway consists of a series of rivers, inland bays, estuaries, sounds, and inlets linked by canals. Vessels are sheltered from the open ocean except for about fifty miles from Boston, along the coast of Rhode Island, and for about thirty-seven miles along the coast of New Jersey.

The completion of the final link in 1939 came just in time for the waterway to provide important service to the nation in World War II. The waterway protected barges carrying much-needed oil and other supplies from enemy submarines lurking off the North Carolina coast.

The "River," as the Brunswick County portion of the waterway is called by the local people, is of enormous economic benefit locally. It becomes especially heavy with traffic twice a year. In the fall a

constant string of boats, large and small, clogs the Waterway, seeking refuge from the wintry blasts of the North.
The vessels present a dazzling parade of chrome, fiberglass,
and varnished teak in their southward progression during
what has come to be known as "the Fall Migration." In the
spring the flow is reversed as boaters seek their summer
nestings.

All year, seemingly endless strings of barges pushed
by small but powerful tugs chug up and down the great
ditch. It is truly marvelous how the tug captains manage
to keep these trains of barges in the narrow channel from
so far in the rear.

The U.S. Atlantic Intracoastal Waterway has contributed a great deal to the nation. It has undoubtedly also
saved the lives of countless commercial and recreational
boaters who, without its existence, would have been exposed to the perils of the open sea.

The waterway near Shallotte Point

The Shallotte waterfront around 1900

Rum Running on the Coast

UNTIL RECENT TIMES, SHALLOTTE, NORTH Carolina, has been a relatively poor area—many of its residents had an extremely tough time making a living. Although the region enjoys increasing affluence these days, there are those who can still remember having to walk to a local business to use the telephone. It's a long way from those times to today's retail stores and cellular phone towers.

Robert (Bobby) Williamson of Shallotte, an eighth- or ninth-generation Milliken on his mother's side, has never lived anywhere else—neither have most of his forebears. Mr. Williamson remembers when Southport was the "deadest place in the world." In the 1950s and '60s, he says, you could "watch the grass grow."

When US Highway 17 was completely paved from Shallotte to Wilmington in 1928, the area changed drastically. Until then, commercial traffic had been mostly by water, with sailboats plying Shallotte Inlet and Southport included in the loop. There was not even a major rail link to southern Brunswick county. But with the new road, Southport and other coastal communities were bypassed, cut off from the main flow of traffic.

This very isolation, however, made the southern Brunswick coast quite suitable for a time for one lucrative enterprise—the transport of bootleg liquor during Prohibition.

According to Mr. Williamson—one of the few willing to tell the tale of his own family's escapades—rum running became big business for the locals during Prohibition. The sailboat captains who formerly would drift or sail from the Shallotte Bridge up to the Wilmington tar yards carrying naval stores found their services in demand for a different cargo.

When nationwide prohibition of alcoholic beverages was enacted at the federal level in 1919 under pressure from religious and social groups (a similar law had already been in effect in North Carolina for a decade), the government found itself in the difficult position of policing miles of coastline and back-country roads to prevent smuggling. With only 1,500 Coast Guard patrolmen and revenue agents assigned to this duty, the feds couldn't hope to prevent all activity.

Along the isolated Brunswick County shore, oceangoing ships would offload cargoes of rum and other spirits from Bermuda or Canada onto waiting sailboats. The local ships would then navigate the local inlets and rivers, going with the tides to a clandestine rendezvous where another faction would see the cartons distributed throughout the area by automobile.

Times had often been hard for working folks in southeastern North Carolina, even in the relatively prosperous 1920s, but the 1929 stock market crash made them worse. The Depression had a devastating effect on the citizens of Brunswick County. For four years Mr. Williamson's father could not find paying work. Farmers got by on subsistence farming for their own tables; you couldn't move

The mouth of the Shallotte River, which was a major commercial route before improved roads.

Kirby's was the main department store in Shallotte for many years.

anything to market, because gasoline was too dear.

So it's perhaps not surprising that some of Brunswick County's most prominent citizens played roles in the rum-running operations. Mr. Williamson recounts one tale involving his grandfather, Capt. Allen Asbury Milliken (whose middle name came from that of the renowned Methodist bishop, Francis Asbury). In March 1928 the captain and his son were caught with eight hundred cases of ill-gotten gain aboard the *George Slover* as they entered Southport Harbor. Someone, it seems, had forgotten to pay off the new harbormaster. The Milliken men pleaded guilty to transportation but never served time.

(In a later incident involving a different sort of illegal substance, the times may change but not the crime: Fifty-odd years later, the sheriff of Brunswick County was arrested and charged with masterminding the importation of marijuana in a similar manner. He and his cronies used shrimp boats to ferry illegal drugs from ships anchored off of Holden Beach; the contraband was then loaded into rental trucks and smuggled into the county. The sheriff and his cohorts did go to prison.)

Mr. Williamson also recalls the story of a 1926 Chevy that wouldn't go in reverse. The automobile was traded for a hog. A few days afterward, when the new owner realized the car was in such bad repair, he returned and demanded his hog back. But it was too late—the hog had already been eaten.

Wider-scale prosperity came to the county in the 1960s, beginning with the creation of recreational golf courses in Boiling Spring Lakes and on Oak Island. The boating and sailing enterprises that once were the cargo-carrying lifeblood of the coast now bring tourist dollars to the region. And a vineyard and winemaking operation, Silver Coast Winery, has brought alcohol production back to the region—quite legally.

Construction of electric utilities in Brunswick County was enabled by Congress's Rural Electrification Act. OPPOSITE: Installation of the first 113 miles of Brunswick's lines began in 1939.

Energized!

IF YOU CAME TO BRUNSWICK COUNTY's beaches much before 1960, chances are you ate your dinner by candlelight. You also warmed the water for your bath on your stove! Public utilities were busy bringing electric service to residents all over the country, but only in areas that made it worthwhile; rural areas like Brunswick County were on the bottom of the list.[8]

Some enterprising locals took advantage of the Rural Electrification Act, passed by Congress in the early 1900s, to sidestep this issue. The legislation allowed Brunswick County to form a cooperative that would link it to other communities, cities that were more densely populated and therefore able to offer more customers per mile of line. The

joint venture kept the cost reasonable while allowing the county to tag on, so to speak.

The local electrical cooperative filed a certificate of incorporation for the Brunswick Electric Membership Corporation (BEMC) with the secretary of state of North Carolina on March 9, 1939. Five months later, a contract with Melvin F. Burgess of Boone, North Carolina, was approved, and the construction of 138 miles of line (113 of them in Brunswick County) began. It doesn't sound like much, but it was a start. Almost five hundred customers came on board and were energized just before the end of the year.

By 1960, more than 10,000 new members signed on, and a new substation was installed to supply power over the

Headquarters of the Brunswick Electric Membership Corporation, near Supply

transmission lines to Shallotte and Midway. The beaches would be next. Oak Island opened a branch office in 1968, just as Carolina Power and Light was announcing their proposed nuclear generating plant in Brunswick County. Things were happening now!

The first load management switch, which allowed BEMC to monitor the amount of power being used, brought state-of-the-art efficiency to the service area of Sunset Beach in 1984. Soon customer service departments and economic development programs had to be implemented—business was booming. The early 1990s brought three incubator locations to facilitate expanding business in the region.

The Brick Landing substation was another milestone for BEMC in June of 1991, bringing the utility to thirty-two substations, with seven transmission and twenty-five distribution stations. The phenomenal growth of Brunswick County, especially in the resort areas, has made BEMC one of the fastest-growing electric cooperatives in North Carolina.

By the end of the twentieth century, BEMC was providing service to 57,000 locations in Brunswick, Robeson, and Bladen Counties—and had become the third largest electric cooperative in the state. In summer or winter, ice or hurricane, we say, "More power to them!"

Headquarters of the Atlantic Telephone Membership Corporation, near Shallotte

Somebody Get the Phone

WHEN YOU LIVE ON A BARRIER ISLAND, it's all about communication. But in most of Brunswick County, until the late 1950s, the best you could do was to use smoke signals or flags. While most of the country had at least a party line established, Brunswick County was struggling to get its telephone cooperative off the ground. Its corporate telecommunications charter was awarded in 1955, and by 1957 the phone company began offering local service. (Southport had already managed to secure separate phone services a few years earlier—the only part of the county con-sidered a priority by the major telephone utility back then!)[9]

Five years later the company had gained a significant number of subscrib-ers—1,400 countywide. With only elev-en employees, the Atlantic Telephone Membership Corporation (ATMC) worked to grow the business and to move to one-party service.

The new phone company grew quick-ly, and by 1978 the operation moved to new headquarters. The services they of-fered expanded as their customer base grew. By the 1980s digital technology was coming on board, and new features such as call waiting and call forwarding became commonplace. Then came cable television, and a whole new system was designed and activated. In 1983 pocket pagers became widely available—and everyone was accessible wherever they went, island or inland.

Pay-per-view television was launched in the 1990s, and the Internet became available via dial-up for all ATMC phone customers. When President Clinton visited Whiteville, in neighboring Columbus County, in the late 1990s, he promised high-speed connections for the schools, and all counties received the benefit of that initiative. DSL (digital subscriber line) service was deployed to an increasingly frustrated community who up to that point had paid long-distances fees for adequate Internet access.

Long distance service was next, followed by Innovative Area Calling Plans. Later a new customer service center was opened at Sunset Beach, and work began on yet another new headquarters. Next on the list for many Brunswick residents is ATMC's new Digital Video Recording (DVR) service. (No more commercials—there is such a thing as too much communication!)

Bringing Brunswick to Your Doorstep

THOUGH IT HAD NO NEWSPAPER of its own until the final years of the nineteenth century, Brunswick County is well served today by the communications media. In addition to the hundreds of network and cable television channels available, two public radio stations provide signal coverage in the area.

Not one but two daily newspapers cover Brunswick County with local editions: The *Wilmington Star-News*, and the *Sun News* out of Myrtle Beach, South Carolina. The *New York Times* and *USA Today* are available at several locations, and newspaper boxes on the beach carry the Charlotte and Raleigh newspapers.

Two outstanding weekly papers are published in Brunswick county: the *State Port Pilot*, which primarily serves southeastern Brunswick County (more specifically Southport, St. James, Boiling Spring Lakes, Bald Head Island, Oak Island, and Caswell Beach) and the *Brunswick Beacon*, serving Shallotte and the South Brunswick Islands.

The *State Port Pilot* was established in 1928, the county's first newspaper to survive more than a few short years (it was preceded by several short-lived papers based in Southport). It was named for the dream of its founder, William B. Keziah—and shared by many citizens of Southport—that their city become North Carolina's principal port. Instead, even though Southport felt it provided many advantages over Wilmington, the state decided to establish Wilmington as its primary port. Southport possesses many assets that could make it a major port (once again, here in the twenty-first century, there is talk of a large port facility and the land has even been purchased and set aside—so maybe the *State Port Pilot* will one day prove

to be aptly named). The *State Port Pilot* provides award-winning coverage of southeastern Brunswick County and the county as a whole.

The *Brunswick Beacon* was established in 1962. The islands of Brunswick County were mostly unpopulated in the early 1960s, and only small communities dotted the surrounding areas. There was scant support for a local newspaper. A series of ill-fated publications dating back to the 1930s discovered this to be a sad fact. The *Beacon*, as it is affectionately called, persevered, and its circulation, size, and advertising revenues grew with the developing area. By the mid-1990s, the *Beacon* had expanded to more than seventy pages. The small weekly newspaper has become the largest weekly broadsheet in North Carolina, and is currently one of the largest in the Southeast. Yes, Brunswick County is a well-read place.

THE WEIRD AND THE WONDERFUL

A Few Brunswick Tales Worth Retelling

Attack of the Carnivorous Plants

YOU MAY BE FAMILIAR WITH THE CARNIVOROUS plant known as the Venus' flytrap, whose feeding habits are a botanical marvel of engineering. But did you know that it's not an exotic import from another country? It's actually native to Southeastern North Carolina—like its carnivorous cousins the pitcher plant and the sundew. One of the only places on earth where these rare species are found naturally is in the Green Swamp of Brunswick County.

The Venus' flytrap is an anomaly among wildflowers. It is readily available for domestic cultivation as a house plant, but it is severely endangered in the wild. The plant feeds through its leaves, which spread out on the ground in moist, spongy soil, circling a single stalk. Each leaf has two blades which are ringed with comblike teeth. The blades are hinged along one side. The bright pinkish color of the inside of the leaf is caused by the thousands of glands which both secrete enzymes and absorb nutrients.

Insects and spiders are attracted by the flytrap's sugary nectar. When they enter and brush against any two of the sensitive hairs along the edge of the leaf, the plant slams shut. The teeth interlock and the prey is trapped. Enzymes then break down the insect's tissue and the plant digests its meal.

The natural population of these plants has been endangered by the removal of them by careless individuals. People interested in having one of their own should remember that they are readily available from reputable retail nurseries. Please leave the wild plants in the wild.

OVERLEAF: The Venus' flytrap secretes a nectar that attracts—and ultimately traps—the insects and spiders it uses for nutrition.

Topsy's Topsy-Turvy Tour Around Town

Years ago, across America, it was a grand occasion when a circus train arrived in town. Almost as soon as the huge tents were set up, a parade began downtown.

The parade might feature caged animals, costumed riders on horseback, a brass band, and a calliope playing carnival music.

One day in October 1922, the Hagenbeck-Wallace circus, one of the largest in the South, arrived in Wilmington, across the river from Brunswick County. It was also the start of a four-day sideshow that alternately terrified, charmed, and amused the town.

On October 9 the circus played to two nearly sold-out crowds under the big tents. That night, following the eight o'clock show, the circus workers, using the elephants for help, struck the tents in a driving rain.

Topsy, a mischievous four-ton Indian elephant, escaped, using the rain and darkness for cover.

A Wilmington police dispatcher received some startling news from an excited caller. "You won't believe this, but there's a varmint in my vegetable garden pulling up my collards with his tail and stuffing them up his rear end and I hope you will come get it," the caller said.

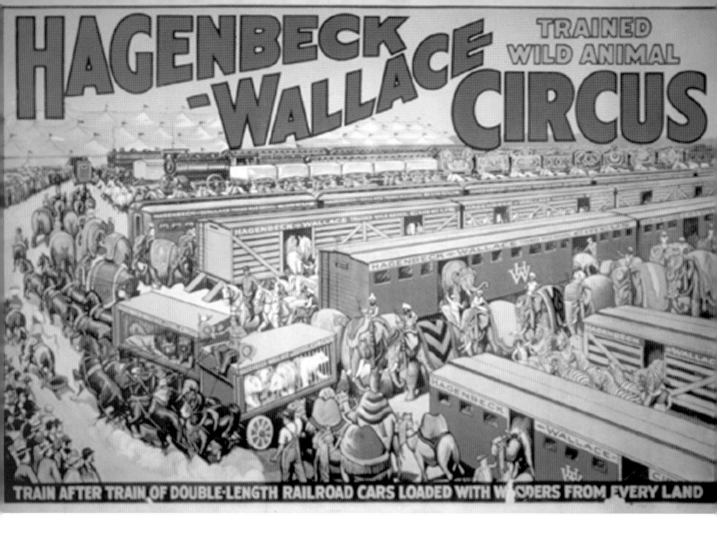

The Hagenbeck-Wallace Circus brought its wild-animal circus acts to towns throughout the United States. Courtesy of Princeton University Library.

But Topsy didn't tarry in the garden. A boarder down the street heard a gate crash and reported "a large gray mule running down the alley between the houses." Another man, feeling his house shake as Topsy tore a pillar from his home, ran into the street, screaming "Earthquake!"

Someone in the eastern part of town saw Topsy in the back yard "wearing a chicken coop and a fence for a yoke." He peppered the elephant with buckshot, and Topsy's wild romp hit high gear.

"It would be impossible to recount every place visited by the elephant," stated a local newspaper, "for the beast went north, south, east and west, followed part of the way by people and police afoot and in automobiles."

Topsy found her way to the Eureka Pressing Club, and may have mistaken her reflected image on a storefront plate glass window for another elephant. Once inside she discovered that it was not so. Topsy made her way to a tub of dye and filled her trunk. She then coolly squirted the compound over suits and garments hanging in the pressing room.

Topsy next crashed through a wall on the side of the building and headed for the mud near the Cape Fear River. She became mired in the muck up to her stomach as she trumpeted with sheer joy and happiness.

Wilmington's finest arrived at this point, and with the use of some endearing words the police persuaded Topsy to move out of the muck.

She extracted herself from the river mud by wrapping her trunk around trees and pulling herself out. Bowing to the temptation of apples, peanuts, and hay, Topsy was led away toward a waiting railroad flatcar.

But Topsy had other ideas. She bolted again, this time diving headfirst into the Cape Fear River and swimming all the way across to the Brunswick County side. There she was again captured, shackled, and loaded onto a train car. Topsy went on to further adventures—but none quite like her visit to southeastern North Carolina.

The Old West or Brunswick County?

ACCORDING TO NEWSPAPER ACCOUNTS of the day, Jesse Walker was "a roving, shiftless fellow." He had deserted from the U.S. Army, he'd been labeled as an outlaw, and he was a suspected burglar.

He was eating his supper when the local sheriff and three of his deputies rode up to his house on horseback and declared their intention to arrest him. What the sheriff and his men did not know was that Jesse had a pistol in his lap under the table.

He stood and began firing at the men. The sheriff took three bullets and a deputy was grazed. The men finally wrestled Jesse to the floor.

A horse and buggy was sent to bring a doctor from the nearest town. The doctor did all that he could, operating by the light of an oil lamp on a kitchen table, but infection set in, and the sheriff died from his wounds.

While this episode may sound like an old Western movie, it all happened near Ocean Isle Beach.

The sheriff, Jackson Stanland, had found success as a dealer in naval stores around the turn of the twentieth century. He was one of the wealthiest landowners in Brunswick County, owning many acres in Shallotte. He was forty-six and had just entered his second term as sheriff when he went to arrest Jesse Walker that Sunday in November 1908.

Stanland had been looking for Walker for more than a week when he heard that Walker had returned to his house at Shallotte Point. According to newspaper accounts, when the sheriff and his men went to apprehend him, Walker fired nine shots, "pouring hot lead at his captors even after his arms were pinned to his side by the grasp of the officers."

When Dr. J. Arthur Dosher was told of the Sheriff's wounds, he came by sailboat from Southport, arriving too late to save Stanland.

Walker and two cohorts were jailed in Southport, only to escape three months later.

J. J. Knox, a former sheriff, put together a posse and followed Walker and his men up the Lockwood Folly River and into the wilds of the Green Swamp. Finally, five days later, after a gunfight, one man was arrested while Walker escaped into the swamp. Six years later, Capt. J. W. Dixon of Southport spotted Walker while eating dinner at a Wilmington restaurant. Dixon tipped off the local police, who arrested Walker stepping off a boat at a Princess Street dock.

In June 1915, Walker was sentenced to thirty years in prison. But four years later he again escaped and was not seen in North Carolina for fifteen years.

Then, on April the 8th, 1935, an old, white-haired man showed up at Central Prison in Raleigh—the state capital—and identified himself as Jesse Walker. He'd come to clear his name and pay his debt to society, he said.

So much time had passed that they had to research prison records to determine his crime and sentence. It is said that after he was released from prison Jesse Walker returned to Shallotte Point—this time as a traveling preacher.

As for Dr. Dosher, he so distinguished himself in the medical profession that Brunswick County's hospital is named for him today.

The Calabash waterfront is still a busy dock for seafood boats, and a popular spot for fresh seafood.

Good Night, Mrs. Calabash, Wherever You Are

THIRTY YEARS AGO, IN A PLACE where the Old Georgetown Road changed course to go around an old live oak tree covered in Spanish moss, the road widened just enough to accommodate access to a few small stores. Nearby, shrimp trawlers would pull up to the docks along the riverfront of the Calabash River to unload the day's catch.

Today the Old Georgetown Road still swerves around that same old oak tree and the shrimp trawlers still pull up to the docks along the riverfront, but now there are more than twenty restaurants serving nearly a million seafood dinners a year. Not many of the visitors to this "Seafood Capital of the World" know the origins of this unique fishing village.

One old-timer, Virgil Coleman, owner of the Calabash Seafood Hut, says it all began with a few oyster shacks down on the riverfront. Then his mother started cooking in their house for the men his father would take out fishing. Lucy Coleman, cooked, while her husband, Curtis, ran the fishing fleet. What they caught, Lucy cooked. Eventually, the Colemans converted their house into a full-fledged restaurant, which Virgil and his brother lease out today as the Original Calabash.

"Calabash style" came to mean seafood that was battered and deep-fried—especially when it was fresh off the boat in this Brunswick County village. The word "calabash" itself refers to a gourd that is often used in cooking or for making African folk musical instruments.

Virgil also recounts one of his mother's stories from the years after World War II when customers first started making their way up to Calabash from the still young resort of Myrtle Beach, South Carolina. It seems there was one customer she remembered for his unusually large nose. He was, she later realized, the famous entertainer Jimmy Durante, and as he left he'd said to her, "Good night, Mrs. Calabash." This phrase would become Durante's trademark farewell, heard by millions of fans at the end of his popular radio shows.

While Lucy Coleman was still cooking at home, her brother-in-law, Vester Beck, opened Beck's, which claims to be the town's first true restaurant.

Then, in 1955, two other families opened Dockside Seafood House, and Thomas's of Calabash Seafood Restaurant soon followed. Since then more than a dozen other restaurants of all types, including a large restaurant named after the renowned old Boundary House, have sprung up.

There are several reasons for the success of these eateries, but mostly it comes down to three things: great seafood, friendly, small-town people, and a family-oriented atmosphere. What made Jimmy Durante decide to use the quirky sign-off may never be known for certain—but no one who's ever dined in the tiny "Seafood Capital" ever forgets its name.

Brunswick waters abound in succulent blue crabs, shrimp, and oysters in season.

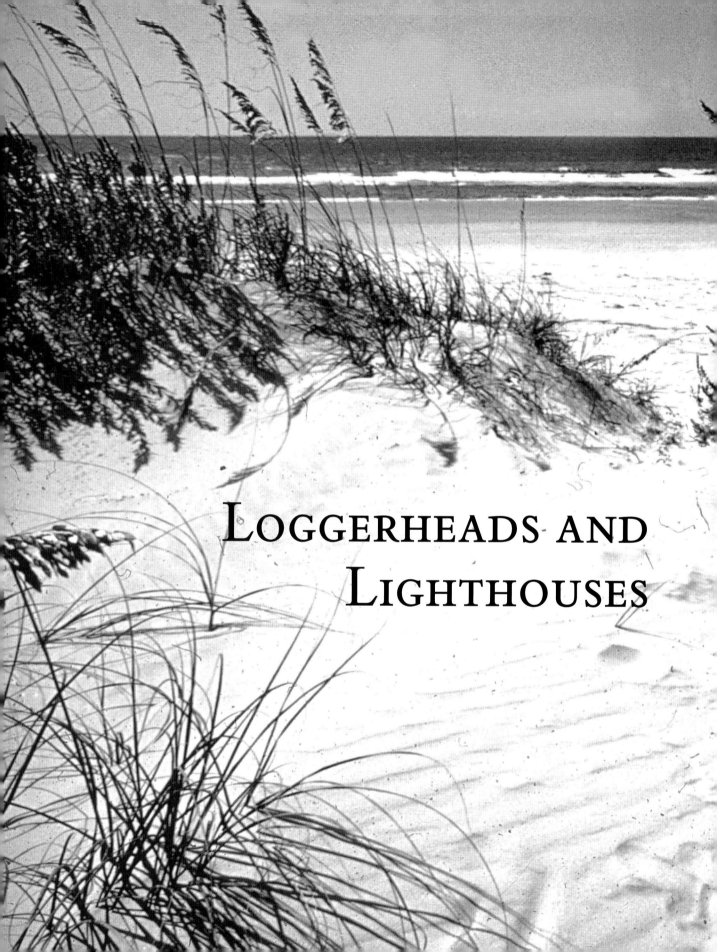

LOGGERHEADS AND
LIGHTHOUSES

Brunswick's Beaches and Waterways

Brunswick and
the Sea

THE PEOPLE OF BRUNSWICK County HAVE always had a close relationship with the sea. Historically, the Atlantic Ocean has provided a livelihood, a method of transportation, and a means of recreation for residents and visitors alike.

For most of Brunswick's history, the ocean has been an important source of food. Shrimp, oysters, clams, and both warm- and cold-water fish have been plentiful. Seafood has also been a chief supplier of income.

Boats built in Brunswick County have sailed the Atlantic and weathered the dangers of the deep, to bring back shrimp for millions of kitchens and restaurants. Prodigious quantities of succulent Brunswick oysters have elated the palates of America's oyster lovers, and mountains of delicious fish have graced the tables of our country.

Until recent decades, the sea was also a principal means of transportation and communication because of the difficulties of movement by road. Boats of all kinds ranged up and down the coast, carrying on all sorts of commerce. From most places in the large county, it was easier to get to the county seat by water than by land.

For generations, places like little Varnamtown near Holden Beach had craftsmen who built sturdy boats, some over one hundred feet in length, by hand, from lumber the builders cut and dried. As hard as it is to believe, these large boats were built without

blueprints. Complex curves were cut by hand, and perfect fits were achieved by an experienced eye.

Unfortunately Brunswick County may have seen the last of these skilled boat builders whose craft was formerly passed on from generation to generation, going back many centuries.

Today the sea is still a source, directly or indirectly, of livelihood for a large part of the population. The

The Atlantic Ocean has long provided Brunswick with a livelihood from the sea, whether in boatbuilding, fishing, or tourism.

attraction of the beaches and the shore has been the catalyst for Brunswick County's thriving tourist industry. It has led to an explosion of golf courses, restaurants, shops, recreational facilities, and new housing developments.

Booming tourism and the vast influx of retirees and new businesses has greatly changed the patterns of employment in Brunswick County. Not only has the population grown at an impressive rate, but the median income has risen dramatically as well.

The people of Brunswick County now enjoy a plethora of services, shopping, and cultural opportunities. The county boasts a state-of-the-art multiplex cinema, a number of museums and art galleries, several bookstores, a system of libraries, numerous cultural associations, a community college, a conference center, and even a planetarium. The region is served by an excellent hospital in Southport as well as medical facilities in Shallotte and the considerable resources of New Hanover County. Many artists and writers have chosen to make their home in Brunswick County as well, further enriching long-established local traditions. All of this commerce and activ-

ity is supplemented by the vast resources of the neighboring cities of Wilmington and Myrtle Beach, which flank Brunswick to the northeast and southwest.

The citizens of Brunswick are served by two small municipal airports, while the nearby international airports of Wilmington and Myrtle Beach open Brunswick County to the world.

Brunswick's waterways are served by two public ferry routes. The vehicle/passenger ferry operated by the North Carolina Ferry Division from Southport to Fort Fisher is the most popular route in the state. The ferry takes about thirty minutes to make a pleasant crossing, providing riders with enjoyable views of marine life, passing watercraft from pleasure boats to oceangoing freighters, and all three of Brunswick's lighthouses.

Passenger ferries are also the only way (besides private boat) to reach Bald Head Island. The privately operated Bald Head Island ferries depart from a terminal on the east side of Southport and take about 25 minutes to reach the island.

Progress, of course, comes at a price. Seafood—while still abundant—is much diminished from what it was in the past, and often threatened by such factors as bacterial runoff and boating traffic. The vast stretches of empty beach are only a memory (a notable exception is Bird Island, a mile-long coastal reserve accessible on foot at low tide from Sunset Beach)—unless you're on the beach in February.

Fishermen of Brunswick still go out to sea in search of shrimp; oysters are still plucked from the shore; but the quaint speech of the past, tinged with Elizabethan accents, is seldom heard anymore, and the sight of a wooden boat or a tall ship rarer still.

The Southport-Fort Fisher ferry is the most heavily traveled route in the North Carolina state ferry system.

What's Going on at the Beach?

An UNMISTAKABLE FEATURE OF Brunswick County is its forty-seven miles of beaches—generally sheltered from the harshest forces of wind and waves by the gentle south-facing curve of the coastline in this part of the state. White-sand beaches line Oak Island and the three other islands—Holden Beach, Ocean Isle Beach, and Sunset Beach—that are collectively known as the South Brunswick Islands.

Human visitors consider Brunswick's beaches mild and welcoming almost all year long. But along this same strand, a community of hardy plants and animals works to find a home in a harsh environment.

The Beach Zone

THE BEACH EXTENDS FROM THE low-tide water level to the "foot" or base of the primary dune. At first it seems to be without life, except for an occasional gull silently standing by the water's edge. Then, from overhead, pelicans and terns dive suddenly to catch surface fishes just beyond the breakers. Offshore, dolphins break the surface as they feed, but on the beach there still appears to be very little activity.[10]

The tidal extremes of the lower beach (the intertidal zone area between low and high tide) create a harsh environment of wet, shifting sands alternating with increased temperature and exposure to drying air. Observers must look carefully to find animal life.

Living on top of the sand is almost impossible, so the inhabitants have adapted to life beneath the sand's surface. Two of the most common of the burrowing animals that dominate this zone are the mole crab and the tiny coquina clam.

The upper beach is the zone between normal high tide and the base of the primary dune. It is an area of shifting sands, intense light and heat, and scant water. The dry sand retains rainwater only briefly, and the air is laden with salt spray.

These factors combine to create a desert-like habitat. Plant life consists of only a few very hardy stragglers from the dune community.

Ghost crabs, one of the principal animals of the upper beach, are easily found here by their many holes in the sand.

Sand dunes protect Brunswick's shoreline from erosion; and sea oats and other vegetation are vital to protecting the dunes.

The Dune Zone

THE DUNE ZONE IS A REGION OF SANDY hills located between the beach and shrub thicket or salt marsh. Like the upper beach, it is very similar to a desert. Every plant and animal living here has adapted to extreme dryness and heat.

Only salt-tolerant species of plants can survive the heavy salt spray and succeed in this zone.

The dunes on Brunswick's beaches are characterized by the presence of sea oats. This rapidly growing salt-resistant plant spreads by seed dispersion and the formation of underground rhizomes. The new plants are a valuable aid in slowing erosion because they stabilize the shifting sand—but it's important not to disturb either new plants or established ones, as they are vital to the stability of fragile dunes.

The Salt Marsh

THE TIDAL WETLANDS FRINGING THE SALTWATER bays and creeks are coastal salt marshes. The lower marsh, or inter-tidal zone, is flooded daily during high tide. This zone is dominated by saltmarsh cordgrass.

Spartina, a sturdy salt-tolerant plant, has adapted to survive alternating periods of exposure to saltwater, sun, and strong winds, as well as the fury of storm-driven waves. Thus it is invaluable as a buffer against eroding wave action. The abundant growth of this cordgrass provides the base of a food chain unsurpassed in variety and richness.

Steps to the Sea

The lowly loggerhead turtles that nest on Southeastern North Carolina beaches descend from reptiles that lived 245 million years ago. There has been little change in their evolutionary makeup as the turtles are perfectly adapted to the aquatic environment of the Brunswick County coast. They are the true natives to our beaches and oceans, swimming now exactly as they did before the first human came to Brunswick's shores.

The only problems they seem to have lie in the reproduction department, as all eight known sea turtle species are either threatened or endangered. Sea turtles inhabit the warm waters of the world, cavorting and floating on the sea currents, with only the females returning to land when it's time to lay their eggs.

A typical adult loggerhead sea turtle weighs in somewhere around 250 pounds. Its reddish-brown carapace, or shell, has a span averaging over three feet in width and up to 45 inches in length. The female is capable of laying 100 eggs at a time. The eggs are the size of ping-pong balls. Translucent and with the consistency of molded Jell-O, they are deposited in a heap in a two-foot nest that the female digs with her back flippers.

The really interesting thing is that the place she chooses to leave her eggs is the same place she herself emerged as a hatchling. How she accomplishes this is one of the incredible mysteries of nature. Somehow on that arduous trek from the dune line to the water's edge, the hatchling imprints indelible data about the turtle's birth beach, and twenty to thirty years later she uses this uncanny information to return to that precise spot.

Nesting season runs from May through early fall, and one female is capable of creating two to three nests per season every other year or so. It's an unending cycle of determining where and when to build her nest and lay her clutch of eggs—making her way first to the right beach, then to the dune line with her huge, lumbering body. All this she does by instinct. She covers it and leaves, never to see a single offspring.

The temperature of the sand determines the sex of the embryos: when the sand is the hottest, more females than males are born. The embryos develop into hatchlings in fifty-five to sixty days, and then on one dark night, a lone scout pokes its tiny head out. If all is clear, this first hatchling uses some secret way of signaling his sisters and brothers before the sand erupts with dozens of baby turtles.

Immediately they head for the water, as if by some internal radar. They use their flippers, dragging first one then the other, building up their muscles and leaving a

Mature loggerhead turtles average 250 pounds, with a carapace (shell) about three feet long.

distinctive pattern in the sand that is reminiscent of bicycle tire tracks.

If the terrain the hatchlings must cross is blocked by something as insignificant as a footprint, the youngsters can easily exhaust themselves trying to get over a ridge. If a ghost crab makes its presence known, the turtle surely won't make it to the sea. Bright lights, such as automobile headlights or street lamps, are known to disorient the young turtles and inadvertently lure them in the opposite direction of the sea.

The journey to the water is the most precarious of the turtle's life; there are many predators, even well-meaning humans can ruin their chances of making it to the sea. Once in the water, the young turtles dive down and ride the undertow to the deeper, safer parts of the sea. But of course, they are prey there, too. Sharks and a multitude of other fish await this tasty delicacy, lowering the odds of survival to only one out of a thousand hatchlings (you do the math, since most nests only have a hundred eggs). Tiny footprints to the sea are all that remain of nests only moments after the hatchlings' nocturnal birth and strenuous journey.

The favorite food of the ones that survive is the common jellyfish. But often trash bags thrown into the sea are mistaken for this food source, and the plastic, once ingested, causes many to die. Then there are the fishnets that may entangle them, collisions with boats, and poachers specifically hunting them for their meat and shells. With the odds so stacked against the sea turtles it is amazing, is it not, that this process has gone on for millions of years?

A Little Island History

As any old-timer will tell you, Ocean Isle was formerly known as Hale's Beach. In earlier days there wasn't much there besides tall, wind-swept dunes, the sea birds, and perhaps a fishing shack or two and some wild goats hanging about. While the beauty of the island was breathtaking, it was not a very comfortable place for folks to stay for long.

In the mid-1950s the island was purchased by Odell Williamson, who undertook the task of laying out the streets and lots and founding a town. At about the same time the first permanent residents, the Sloane family, moved there and in 1956 established the first real estate office on the island.

Times have changed; Ocean Isle Beach has been "discovered," yet the island maintains the quiet charm and beauty that brought the first homeowners here half a century ago. It is still a family beach, welcoming those from the big cities in need of a respite from the hectic pace of their lives.

The Ocean Isle Bridge is one of the high-rise bridges constructed to provide access to Brunswick's barrier islands after 1984.

Guiding Lights and Rescuers

Fans of lighthouses and other guiding lights can find a lot to love in Brunswick County, which is home to a number of lighthouses, a U.S. Life-Saving station, and even, in times past, a lightship.

Old Baldy

THE BALD HEAD LIGHTHOUSE, AFFECTIONATELY KNOWN as Old Baldy, is North Carolina's oldest surviving lighthouse. The current structure is not the island's first beacon; an earlier light was built in 1795, but, constructed too close to the water, it fell victim to erosion problems and was demolished by 1810.

The 109-foot-tall Old Baldy was constructed about a mile from the ocean in 1817 to illuminate Frying Pan Shoals, a dangerous stretch of shoals that extends more than thirty nautical miles out into the Atlantic. Its light was visible for about eighteen miles, never sufficient to completely illuminate the shoals.

In January 1865 the Confederate forces disabled Old Baldy prior to losing control of the Cape Fear River in the battle at Fort Fisher.

In the early 1900s the Bald Head light was downgraded to a low-intensity, steady light and was finally discontinued in 1935. From 1941 to 1958 Old Baldy produced a radio beacon to direct ships into the Cape Fear River channel in times of fog and bad weather. Today, it emits a long steady beam as a restored historical site.

"Old Baldy" is North Carolina's oldest surviving lighthouse, while the Oak Island Lighthouse (overleaf) is one of the nation's newest.

Price's Creek Lighthouse is the last surviving Civil War–era lighthouse on the Cape Fear River.

Price's Creek Lighthouse

IN 1848 THE UNITED STATES Congress authorized the construction of eight lighthouses along the Cape Fear River to illuminate the twenty-five mile stretch between Oak Island and Wilmington. The brick shell known as Price's Creek Lighthouse, located hear the Southport ferry landing on what is today privately owned land, is the only one of the original eight still standing.

Price's Creek Lighthouse, only twenty feet tall, was the smaller of two lights originally located at Price's Creek. Two other lighthouses were constructed on Oak Island, two were built at Upper Jettee, and the last two were situated at Orton's Point and at Campbell's Island.

Between the Price's Creek and Federal Point lighthouses, a lightboat was placed at Horseshoe Shoal.

Price's Creek Lighthouse served as a Confederate signal station during the Civil War. It helped blockade runners navigate the river and also aided the shore batteries in identifying the blockade runners.

As the Confederates lost control of the Cape Fear River, they destroyed all the river lights to keep them from falling into enemy hands, hoping to impede Union navigation.

By the late 1880s, unattended beacons had replaced all of the river lights. Today, Price's Creek Lighthouse is not accessible to the public. The lighthouse is missing its glass-and-iron lamp top, but the property owner has repaired the Civil War cannon damage and structural decay. The lighthouse can be seen from the ferry between Fort Fisher and Southport as the ferry approaches the Southport landing.

Oak Island Lighthouse

OAK ISLAND LIGHTHOUSE, constructed in 1958, was one of the last lighthouses built in America. It is the last manually operated lighthouse in the world.

As in the case of the Price Creek Lighthouse, Oak Island originally had two beacons, part of the series of navigational lights designed to guide ships up the river to Brunswick Town and Wilmington.

The original beacons were intended to help with navigation by allowing approaching ships to line them up. Unfortunately, they had not been properly placed. During the Civil War both lights were destroyed. They were rebuilt in 1879, but a hurricane in 1893 seriously damaged the front beacon. The following year their use was discontinued.

The present lighthouse is 153 feet high. It was constructed with an eight-inch-thick reinforced concrete base anchored with twenty-four pipe pilings. The pilings are filled with concrete to a depth of sixty-seven feet. This design allows the tower to sway about three inches in a 100-mile-per-hour wind. The color compounds mixed into the original concrete reduces maintenance—the light's three distinct stripes never need painting.

The eleven-foot-tall aluminum lantern on top of the tower was placed by two helicopters.

The Oak Island Lighthouse is one of the most powerful lighthouses in the world. Its 4,000-watt aerobeam lights can be seen twenty-four miles out to sea. A second bank of lights is used as backup. The lighthouse's characteristic flash pattern is four flashes every ten seconds, with 2,500,000 candlepower.

Members of the U.S. Coast Guard act as lightkeepers and make weekly inspections, climbing the 120 narrow metal steps to the platform and a fourteen-rung metal ladder to the lantern room. The light is turned on each evening thirty minutes before sunset, and off each morning thirty minutes after sunrise.

The service provided by the lighthouse, though it is useful, is no longer considered vital. The National Park Service and the U.S. General Services Administration approved the gift of the lighthouse to the town of Caswell Beach in 2003. This transfer ensures that the lighthouse will remain in local control with proper preservation.

U.S. Life-Saving Station at Oak Island

THE LIFE-SAVING STATION ON OAK Island was one of about 280 such structures erected along America's shorelines. Built in 1889 from standard 1882-style plans drawn by federal architects, and constructed by local builders, the station is one of the few like it still standing today.[11]

During the eighteenth century the United States government became increasingly concerned with the safety of cargoes and passengers being transported at sea. America's vast coastlines, especially the barrier islands of North Carolina, posed hazards for sailing ships. But it was not until the 1870s that humanitarian concerns finally moved the government to formally establish a life-saving service to aid shipwreck victims. In the 1880s, at last, stations were built at key points south of Hatteras Inlet.

The stations were situated to allow regular beach patrols on foot as well as observation from towers, and they were often built near lighthouses. The station at Oak Island occupied the tip of the island past Fort Caswell, and although there were no roads to that end of the island, the station could be reached by boat from nearby Smith Island (now known as Bald Head Island). Crews of surfmen held watch day and night during the storm season, scanning the surf for disabled vessels or searching the beach for evidence of new wrecks. The surfmen carried red cotton flares to signal a boat in trouble or to summon help.

Surfboats were mounted from the rafters in the station and a beach cart for rescue apparatus was stored ready for action. A Lyle gun, a type of small cannon, could be

hauled to the site of a wreck and used to fire a projectile carrying a lifeline out to stranded mariners. The crew and passengers could then be carried to shore in the breeches buoy (a life ring with a canvas seat, attached to a pulley) or loaded into a surfboat. Even in smooth seas a rescue operation was difficult; it was especially risky at night in a storm. But the lifesaving crews mounted valiant efforts and pulled off many heroic rescues which were matter-of-factly recorded in the stations daily log books. One Oak Island keeper, Dunbar Davis, helped save people from five shipwrecks in a single day during an 1893 hurricane.

After the station was decommissioned in 1940, the building was moved across the street and eventually sold. Most of the infrastructure has been updated by civilian owners. The original station did not even have any indoor plumbing; however, it was built so sturdily that it was one out of only five structures left standing on Oak Island after Hurricane Hazel in 1954.

The historical building that played such an active role in coastal rescue is one of five remaining 1882-style life-saving stations in the country, and the only one whose tower is in near-mint condition. It was purchased in 1999 by former Midwesterners Gary and Judy Studer, who have turned its restoration into a labor of love. What a thrill it must be to live in a home that has seen so much history, and to live in the very same quarters once occupied by rescuers who stood watch along the corridor now known as the Graveyard of the Atlantic.

Frying Pan Shoals Light Tower and Lightship

THE FRYING PAN SHOALS LIGHT Tower sits in forty feet of water at the merging point of the Cape Fear River and the Atlantic Ocean, twenty-eight miles offshore.

Built in 1964, its towers rise forty feet above the water. The station was completely automated, with a foghorn, a radio beacon, and an automated light that is visible for seventeen miles.

From 1854 to 1964, before the light tower, a lightship was anchored at the shoals. The lightship—a manned vessel—was deemed impractical because of hurricanes, and its was replaced by the light tower, which did not involve such a risk to human life.

The decommissioned lightship *Frying Pan* (designated LV 115) is still in existence, one of thirteen lightships remaining from more than a hundred built for the U.S. Coast Guard. From 1930 to 1965 it guarded its namesake, Frying Pan Shoals, off of Cape Fear. She is 133 feet 3 inches long and 30 feet wide, and weighs 632 gross tons. Now permanently docked at a pier on the Hudson River in New York City, the *Frying Pan* serves as an entertainment venue. Originally put into service in 1930, the ship is listed on both the New York State and Federal Registers of Historic Places.

Lightships were used by the Coast Guard as floating lighthouses. They prevented other ships from running aground on shoals or submerged rocks that were too far from land to be served by a lighthouse on shore.

The entrances to many harbors were marked by lightships. The hulls of these

A lightship—a floating beacon—warned mariners away from the dangerous shoals at the mouth of the Cape Fear River from 1854 to 1964.

ships were designed with a unique shape to withstand the numerous storms and hurricanes that required other ships to seek safe harbor.

A crew of fifteen kept the light atop the mast burning and the foghorn sounding regardless of the weather, season, or time of day. The men remained aboard for three months then received two months of shore leave. It was a job, according to one report, "filled with months of boredom followed by minutes of pure fear."

The old lightship *Frying Pan* has led a remarkable life. Retired in 1965 and donated for a museum exhibit in Southport, she lay for years at anchor, rusting, first in North Carolina and then at an old oyster cannery in Chesapeake Bay. The ship was sold in 1984 but sank on her way northward—probably due to a broken pipe after being abandoned for so long.

The *Frying Pan* was raised and salvaged three years later, and sold to its present owner instead of being scrapped. Tons of silt and shells were removed from the hull, and a new engine was installed. The old ship was then sailed to Manhattan, where she rests at her current home at the Chelsea Piers. The outside has been largely restored to its original appearance, but she remains rusted and barnacle-encrusted on the inside—no deterrent to the edgy musical performances and parties she hosts today.

The Frying Pan Shoals Light Tower, which has marked the mouth of the Cape Fear River since 1963, is destined to be dismantled and used as an artifical reef. Its navigational and weather functions were taken over in 2003 by a new data buoy.

Exploring the Silver Coast Today

Sights and Sites in Brunswick and Beyond

An Old-Timer

CERTAIN ENDURING IMAGES INSTANTLY EVOKE thoughts of the old South: stately, columned plantation homes; paddle-wheel riverboats; and most important, long avenues lined with live oaks dripping with Spanish moss.

In Brunswick County, the live oak (also the state tree) is the predominate hardwood species.

Live oaks are different from other oak trees, many of which lose their large leaves in the fall and grow new ones in the spring. Live oaks, however, remain green all year and grow to immense proportions. The Southern live oak, which thrives here, is one of two varieties (the other is the California live oak). These trees can live for hundreds of years, and the old ones are a truly magnificent sight. At Orton Plantation and several other long-established properties, grand oak alleys survive.

Gause Landing, west of the entrance to Ocean Isle Beach, features some beautiful old specimens. At Shallotte Point near Village Point Road is a truly ancient live oak, believed by locals to be around two thousand years old! It is really something to stand beside a living thing so old.

Gardens of Earthly Delights

AMONG THE BEAUTIFUL GARDENS IN THE Brunswick area just waiting to be enjoyed are Orton Plantation and Gardens, on the River Road between Southport and Wilmington, and Airlie Gardens near Wrightsville Beach east of Wilmington.

Orton Plantation, situated on the Cape Fear River, was once a leading rice plantation. Orton House, built in 1725, is a perfect example of southern antebellum architecture. Over the years various owners have planted avenues of live oak trees, constructed terraces overlooking the old rice fields and river, and imported camellias, azaleas, banana shrubs, and other ornamentals as well as flowering bulbs.

Some gardens were designed to be formal, while others have been left natural to take advantage of the impressive oaks and other native trees. Vast lawns, impressive water fountains, and pleasant walkways were constructed to add to the appeal of formal and natural gardens.

In nearby Wilmington, Airlie Gardens was formerly the estate of Pembroke Jones, a wealthy Wilmingtonian with interests in rice and railroads, and his wife, Sarah Wharton Green. The grounds overlook picturesque Money Island on Wrightsville Sound, where Captain Kidd reputedly buried his treasure. Today the 67-acre property is owned by New Hanover County and is open to the public.

As visitors walk through Airlie Gardens, they pass down a winding road bordered by stately magnolias, azaleas, and rare camellia varieties. On each side of the roadway, majestic moss drapes from the branches of live oaks, some of the largest specimens in the South. Continuing, visitors come to a bridge spanning a placid artificial lake built by the Joneses in 1902. The view from the bridge is breathtaking. Just beyond the bridge is a jasmine-covered stone pergola where graceful white swans float upon tranquil waters.

Brookgreen Gardens. located a short drive south of Brunswick County on US 17, has been called "the floral jewel of South Carolina's coastal community." It was established in 1931 by Archer Huntington and his wife, sculptor Anna Hyatt Huntington, founded Brookgreen Gardens to preserve the native flora and fauna and display objects of art within that natural setting.

ABOVE: Wilmington's historic Arlie Gardens is home to thousands of azaleas, camellias, and other plantings amid the live oaks beside Bradley Creek. RIGHT: Brookgreen Gardens, south or Myrtle Beach, South Carolina, features original sculptures in a formal garden setting.

Today, the 9,200-acre Brookgreen Gardens is a National Historic Landmark. Within its boundaries may be found a breathtaking collection of outdoor sculpture, a 250-year-old live-oak allée, a rich formal garden featuring year-round beauty, and a diverse mix of forested swamps, salt marsh, sandy ridges and fresh tidal swamps. Boat tours of the Waccamaw River offer a close-up view of wildlife and plants and the history of the area's rice culture.

Both Orton Plantation and Airlie Gardens are open from the beginning of March, through the summer and into the fall. Brookgreen is open year round.

The Carolina Bays

Approximately eight miles south of Shallotte, on US Highway 17, densely overgrown woods flank the road on both sides. If you were to fly over in an airplane, or struggle through the growth on foot, you would be one of a few people to see Dog Head Bay. A bay in the middle of woods? On top of a hill? No, not a body of water; we're talking about Carolina bays.

Scattered along the southeastern coast of the United States are approximately 500,000 elliptically shaped depressions in the landscape known as Carolina bays.

The origin of these shallow basins of various sizes has been disputed since the bays were first recognized from aerial photographs during the 1930s. There have been at least sixteen different hypotheses involving terrestrial or extraterrestrial processes offered as explanations for the creation of the bays.

One theory suggests that a meteor hit Earth thousands of years ago, breaking into pieces that made dents as they skipped across the planet's surface. Then there's the legend that Carolina bays are dinosaur footprints (this one has definitely been ruled out). Researchers believe Carolina bays to be at least 30,000 to 100,000 years old, yet scientists are not certain of their origins.

Researchers do know this much: Carolina bays are isolated wetlands in natural, shallow depressions that are largely fed by rain and shallow ground water. The bays all have an elliptical shape and generally a northwest-to-southeast orientation. They are found primarily in the Carolinas and Georgia but range from Florida to Delaware.

Carolina bays vary in size from less than an acre to many acres. Lake Waccamaw, a popular recreational lake in neighboring Columbus County, is the largest of the bay lakes on the North Carolina coastal plain.

The term "bay lake" originates from the abundance of bay trees growing in the many swampy, oval depressions on the Carolina coastal plain.

Some people consider Carolina bays to be annoying wet spots. Farmers commonly plowed through them, and builders filled and paved over them until federal wetlands regulations began protecting them in the mid-1970s. More than 97 percent of the Carolina bays once found in South Carolina have been destroyed or severely altered.

A recent *Smithsonian Magazine* article points out that scientists are discovering flora and fauna in individual bays that are unique to each bay, found nowhere else in the world.

In the 1930s, aerial surveys of North and South Carolina revealed the pattern of Carolina bays.

Mysteries, Ghosts, and Black Waters

THE VISITORS WHO COME TO Brunswick County are usually concerned most with enjoying the area's beautiful beaches or following the elusive white, dimpled ball around a signature golf course. But if they stick only to the well-trodden tourist paths, they may overlook other attractions nearby—some beautiful, some eerie.

The dark, mysterious rivers that drain the Green Swamp can be fascinating places to go boating. The Waccamaw, Lockwood Folly, and Shallotte Rivers offer quiet inlets and backwaters not readily spotted from the road. Largemouth bass, chain pickerel, crappie, and bream lurk beneath the surface of tea-colored waters, awaiting the ea-ger angler. A trip down a local stream with a guide can also introduce wonderful avian worlds. Hawks, ducks, and shorebirds can be seen everywhere. The Green Swamp it-self, a dense pocosin thicket, is a habitat for species of warblers, towhees, and sparrows, and wood ducks.

Some of these same rivers are home to alligators, although you have to look close-ly to see them, as they blend in so well (in most instances they are more afraid of you than you are of them, but you won't want to disturb an alligator if you do come upon one). Yes, there are snakes in these black-water rivers—but poisonous reptiles are rarely encountered.

The waters of southeastern North Carolina are home to alligators, ducks and other waterfowl, and many small mammals, among other species.

Ghosts of Calamities Past

IF YOU ARE INFATUATED WITH ghosts and strange phenomena, you don't have to visit an ancient castle in Great Britain or even an abandoned mansion in New England to find one. Brunswick County has just the thing, with one of this country's most famous ghosts.

The headless ghost is known in these parts as Joe Baldwin, a brakeman on the east-west railroad line that traversed the northern part of Brunswick County in the nineteenth century.

As legend has it, poor old Joe lost his noggin in a train accident one night in the spring of 1867. On that night the last car of Joe's train became separated from the engine and the rest of the train just outside of the tiny town of Maco as it neared its final destination of Wilmington. Unfortunately, another train was close behind Joe's train. He ran to the back of the car, frantically waving his lantern as the uncoupled car decelerated, and he could see the cyclops eye of the train behind rapidly approaching. Joe bravely waved his lantern until the last, but his efforts tragically failed to warn off the other train. Baldwin was decapitated when the second train collided with the car.

Soon after the accident, lovers who had been strolling near the railroad at night reported seeing a strange light along the tracks. The apparition had started with just a flicker over the left rail about a mile from Maco Station. It had approached, growing brighter as it came up the track. It seemed to advance faster and faster, swinging from side to side. Then after a pause it started backwards. Briefly it hung suspended where it had first appeared. Then it was gone.

Over the years watchers have reported seeing the Maco Light. Many believe it is Joe Baldwin's lantern, as the trainman searches for his head. Even though the light was once absent for over a month it always came back. Dark, rainy nights seemed to be Joe's preference.

There have always been skeptics. After paved highways were constructed in the area, they maintained that the light was merely a reflection. An attempt was made to resolve the reflection theory in the mid-1900s. A group of observers watched for the light while all traffic in the area was blocked off. They saw Joe's lantern swinging as usual.

A short time before that, the ghostly lantern had eluded a company of Fort Bragg soldiers armed with rifles, who had decided to end Joe's nightly excursions.

Joe Baldwin is a very special ghost: he has the distinction of having been seen by a president of the United States. President Grover Cleveland saw his light in 1886.

As long as the railroad ran, signalmen at Maco used two lanterns, one red and one green—because over the years railroad engineers sometimes mistook Joe's light for a real signal.

The Maco Light has been seen by many people over the years, though reports grew fewer after the train tracks were removed in the 1990s. The mystery of what causes the light has never been solved.

Maco is located twelve miles northwest of Wilmington on US Highway 74/76; the old railroad crossing is located a short distance outside of town.

An equally tragic but less spectacular local ghost is said to reside in the Brunswick Inn in Southport.

According to folklore, the ghost of musician Antonio Caseletta roams the old Inn, which dates back to 1857. Festive balls were frequently hosted there in the 1880s, and Caseletta was a visiting Italian harpist who played at the inn in 1882. He drowned while sailing off Bald Head Island that same year. The morning after the accident, guests claimed that the strings of the musician's harp had been ripped out. Tony has made the inn his home ever since!

Another mystery that hasn't been solved is the fate of the settlers of the Lost Colony. A group of people living in the swamps near Battle Royal believe that they are their descendants. They call themselves the Roe Nokers, and their dialect is much the same as that which was spoken during the time of Queen Elizabeth I and Sir Walter Raleigh.

A few hours spent visiting the Old Smithville Burying Ground in Southport will unlock pages from the history of Brunswick County, and give you an even better understanding of the events that shaped early America. The cemetery was incorporated in 1749, although some burials took place earlier.

A Tale of Two Cities

BRUNSWICK COUNTY HAS THE GOOD fortune to be situated close to two distinctly different, large cities, each located only a few miles away

Myrtle Beach, South Carolina, one of the largest resorts in the country, reverberates with the pulse of big-time entertainment. Visitors can choose from shows and concerts at venues ranging from the Alabama Theater to the House of Blues, from Dolly Parton's Dixie Stampede to the multifaceted Broadway at the Beach.

Highrise motels and condominiums line Myrtle Beach's oceanfront, while mile after mile of amusements line the highways. Golf courses and outlet stores are plentiful, along with restaurants by the thousands. White-sand beaches, a state park, and numerous waterways provide even more opportunities for outdoor recreation.

The place called "Myrtle Beach" is really more of a geographic center than a city. The city of Myrtle Beach is only a part of the Grand Strand, a strip of coastline more than fifty miles long that runs from Georgetown at the south end to Little River at the North Carolina border. If it's action you want, this is the place!

North on US Highway 17 and across the Cape Fear Memorial Bridge lies the city of Wilmington—the twenty-first-century version of the upstart town that toppled Brunswick Town from political influence in the 1700s. Wilmington exudes old, historic southern charm. Historic markers in the well maintained historic district line the streets, proclaiming Wilmington's association with a myriad of famous people from Whistler's mother to Woodrow Wilson to Mary Baker Eddy, founder of the Christian Scientist Church.

Many of Wilmington's historic buildings and antebellum mansions are open to visitors. Thalian Hall is the city's historic opera house (sharing space with its City Hall); Thalian Hall is the only original surviving theater designed by John W. Tremble, America's greatest theater architect. He also designed the original Ford's Theater in Washington, D.C., where Lincoln was shot.

The Burgwin-Wright house was used as headquarters of Gen. Cornwallis during the American Revolution—before the general went on to lay down his sword at Yorktown, Virginia, and to later become the viceroy of India.

The film industry blossomed in southeastern North Carolina in the early 1980s, and today Wilmington boasts the largest movie sound stage in the U.S. outside of Hollywood. Everything necessary for production—from casting companies to catering and electrical suppliers to stretch limos for the big stars—can be found here. It's not unusual to spot a movie or television show filming on location around town. On a walking or bus tour, visitors might even spot a celebrity.

Wilmington has managed to preserve its small-town atmosphere while becoming a surprisingly cosmopolitan city. It has many excellent restaurants and rich cultural opportunities.

A Sunny Horizon

TODAY, ONE OF NORTH CAROLINA'S ONCE POOREST and most isolated counties is on the move. It is now home to far more than its share of artists, craftsmen, and writers. The people of Brunswick still farm and fish—but they also produce computer software, design and print brochures and ads, send out global positioning devices to the world, and engage in other high-tech pursuits.

A one-lane swing bridge has connected Sunset Beach to the mainland for years.

There are museums, art galleries, branches of major department stores, restaurants of almost every description and cuisine, a college, a nucelar power plant, a community theater company, numerous medical facilities, a U.S. military ocean terminal, a major conference center, and even a planetarium.

Brunswick County has been blessed with a wonderful climate—mild enough, especially along the coast, to grow many varieties of palm trees and tropical plants but with four seasons to break the monotony. Brunswick gets many more hours of annual sunshine than most of the country, yet has abundant greenery. There are miles and miles of beaches and waterways, and recreational opportunities abound.

Once in a while Mother Nature gets bored with tranquility and unleashes her wrath of wind and tide to keep Brunswick from being too perfect. While many South Carolina hurricanes don't spare the rod, the unique geography of Cape Fear protects Brunswick County from most North Carolina hurricanes. Once in a while, though, Brunswick receives a good spanking due to the counterclockwise spin of Atlantic hurricanes—witness Hurricane Hazel in 1954, the worst storm in memory for most southeastern North Carolinians.

As the twenty-first century unfolds for Brunswick County new opportunities and challenges arise. Much is being gained while much is also being lost. For this author, however, who has seen a right good bit of the planet, Brunswick County remains one of the fairest portions of the Earth under heaven.